recent study of New York City
ꜰh school students showed that 80
rcent drank to some extent,
d that *12 percent could be classed
problem drinkers!*

ꜰhen Massachusetts lowered the legal
ꜰnking age to 18 in 1973, the number
fatal highway accidents involving
n-agers increased *167 percent*
the next 18 months!

California it has been estimated that
ꜰre than 25 chapters of Alcoholics
ꜰonymous are now primarily
ꜰnducted by members under the age
21—and the number is growing
a frightening rate!

ꜰese are only a few of the shocking
ꜰdences that the authors have
ꜰembled on the fastest-growing
ꜰrcotic problem in America today.

ꜰoblem drinking among teen-agers
ꜰs reached a level many experts
ꜰnsider to be of epidemic proportions.
ꜰe to easy accessibility of booze,
ꜰe lack of legal penalties for use or
ꜰssession, the greed of the alcohol
ꜰlustry whose "soda-pop wines"
ꜰe aimed directly at the young, and—
ꜰimarily—the permissive attitudes of
ꜰrents who refuse to see alcohol
ꜰan addictive narcotic, we may be
ꜰating a generation of alcoholics.

ꜰe problem is real, and it is growing
every part of America every day.
ꜰrough interviews with experts
the field, analysis of the scientific
ꜰta, and rap sessions with hundreds of
ꜰn-age drinkers and their parents,
ꜰe Addeos have built a frightening
ꜰcture—and provided sound advice for
ꜰ adults who must deal with the
ꜰoblem of adolescent drinking.

EDMOND G. ADDEO has been a
professional athlete, editor, journalist,
and novelist. He is the co-author of
The Midnight Special (a fictional
biography of Leadbelly), *Egospeak—
Why No One Listens To You* and
*Inside Divorce—Is It What You Really
Want?*

JOVITA REICHLING ADDEO is a
registered nurse, a mother, and an
active participant in local drug
programs. The Addeos live in
Mill Valley, California, with their
two teen-age daughters.

WHY OUR CHILDREN DRINK

Other books by
Edmond G. Addeo

EGOSPEAK:
WHY NO ONE LISTENS TO YOU

INSIDE DIVORCE—
IS IT WHAT YOU REALLY WANT?

WHY OUR
CHILDREN
DRINK

by Edmond G. Addeo
and
Jovita Reichling Addeo

Introduction by Dr. Morris E. Chafetz, Director
National Institute
on Alcohol Abuse and Alcoholism

PRENTICE-HALL, INC.,
Englewood Cliffs, N.J.

Why Our Children Drink
by Edmond G. Addeo and Jovita Reichling Addeo

Printed in the United States of America

Prentice-Hall International, Inc., London
Prentice-Hall of Australia, Pty. Ltd., Sydney
Prentice-Hall of Canada, Ltd., Toronto
Prentice-Hall of India Private Ltd., New Delhi
Prentice-Hall of Japan, Inc., Tokyo

10   9   8   7   6   5   4   3   2   1

Library of Congress Cataloging in Publication Data
Addeo, Edmond G
    Why our children drink.
    1. Alcohol and youth—United States.   2. Liquor
problem—United States. I. Addeo, Jovita Reichling,
joint author.   II. Title.
HV5135.A33   362.2′92′0973   75-20326
ISBN-0-13-959460-4

For Denise and Nicole —

may all your highs be natural ones

Introduction

For several years now, a great deal of attention has been given—both in the mass media and in the professional literature—to evidence of increased alcohol use and misuse among adolescents. It was inevitable that these reports would rouse strong interest, since they reach directly into a primary concern of millions of people—their own family life and the welfare of their teen-age and preteen children.

Fortunately, parents are not alone in their concern about the dynamics of alcohol use by the young. People in such fields as government, education, social services, and youth-oriented organizations are engaged in attempts to obtain increasingly more accurate information about teen-age drinking, to develop sensible reactions to it, and to establish effective programs for minimizing the problems it causes.

In this context, *Why Our Children Drink,* by Edmond and Jovita Addeo, fulfills a real need. Aimed primarily at parents, it nevertheless surveys a range of matters which are of interest in helping professionals in various areas as they study the phenomena of teen-age drinking and teen-age problem drinking. Like many books which come to grips with complicated and emotion-laden issues, the present work presents the authors' own conclusions, drawn from an array of independent reports. The issues related to alcohol and young people demand further consideration and debate; one hopes that ensuing discussions will be based on the same kind of wide-ranging review that underpins *Why Our Children Drink.*

Among the many problems which come within the purview of the National Institute on Alcohol Abuse and Alcoholism, I feel a special urgency in the area of alcohol and young people.

Simply put, the taking of alcohol is basically an adult activity, since it is the taking of a drug. Yet alcohol use by adolescents is definitely increasing.

Various studies have indicated that experimentation with

alcohol has become almost universal among high school students; that the number of regular drinkers, the quantity of alcohol consumed, and the frequency of use in this population increase proportionately with age; and that these trends have been accelerating. The preliminary results of a national survey conducted for the National Institute early in 1974 indicated that 93 percent of boys and 87 percent of girls in their senior year of school had experimented with alcohol, and more than half of the nation's seventh graders had tried drinking at least once during the previous year.

Problem drinking among young people shows a similar pattern of increase. Of course, problem drinking by adolescents may not have the same meaning as problem drinking by adults. As the *Second Special Report to the U.S. Congress on Alcohol and Health from the Secretary of Health, Education, and Welfare* (1974) pointed out, "According to some criteria, any drinking by an adolescent may be defined as a problem. If we adopt a problem-drinking criterion of getting 'high' or 'tight' at least once a week, preliminary estimates from the 1974 survey indicate that approximately 5 percent of the students are problem drinkers. By a less conservative criterion of getting drunk four or more times a year, approximately 23 percent of the students exhibited potential problem-drinking signs."

The fact that taking alcohol is basically an adult activity is one of the principal reasons why young people drink, viewing it as a mark of maturity which an adolescent yearns for. Similarly, the fact that so many adults drink irresponsibly is a prime factor in adolescent problem drinking, since role modeling by adults often shows *how* the activity is done. This is true not only in the tragic and frequent cases of children who ultimately follow a parent into clinical alcoholism, but also among the countless more who learn from their own parents that the very purpose of drinking is to get "a little high."

Even without such directly damaging examples, parents

often send their children a confusing batch of signals about taking alcohol—signals which reflect the parents' own ambivalence and confusion about drinking. Naturally, the inevitable result is ambivalence and confusion in the next generation. This chain must be broken, as adults form a clear, rational approach to alcohol, choosing to use it moderately or not at all.

Parents sending their children clear, healthy messages about alcohol use and nonuse will, of course, be only one of the forces forming these young people's attitudes and behavior, but parents are a powerfully significant force. Even though confusing, ambiguous messages will still be sent to the youngsters from the adult society around them, the parental influence can be decisive, especially if it is backed up by low-key, factual educational efforts in the school and elsewhere.

I was delighted to see that the authors of the present work place much emphasis on the development of responsible decision making about alcohol use and on parents' need to define their own thinking and habits in this area. The efforts of the National Institute on Alcohol Abuse and Alcoholism in the prevention of alcohol problems among young people focus largely on such factors, since the teen-agers' decisions about alcohol emerge from their total value system. Learning about alcohol and deciding about alcohol use are not done in isolation from other learning and deciding. Too often, an attempt has been made to place alcohol matters into such isolation, even in the form of "Do as I say, not as I do." Whether in the home, the school, a youth organization, or elsewhere, this will not work. Hysteria about alcohol use among the young leads to "education" efforts in isolation; a concern based on objective facts leads to integrated efforts at the development of rational choices in this matter as in others.

Some perceptive observers have noted that the much-feared, much-cited "peer pressure" among adolescents actually includes, in many cases, pressure *not* to drink excessively. It should not be surprising that many teen-agers have a value system which does not include overdosing with alcohol, and that they feel scorn for drunken behavior when they encounter it. Integrated, thought-out value systems are not, after all, a new thing in human life. Our task is to foster them and to work for the integration of drinking decisions within them.

Dr. Morris E. Chafetz, Director
National Institute of Alcohol Abuse and Alcoholism

Acknowledgements

Listing the professional individuals, organizations, local agencies, and teen-agers around the country who all helped in gathering and evaluating material for this book, would probably require a book in itself. Some people, such as Art Cole, youth counselor in the Los Angeles area, Claudia Sampson and her San Mateo Youth Advisory Council, or Wendy Menard and Emanda Miller with the Michigan and Los Angeles A.S.A.P., respectively—and certainly Dr. Morris Chafetz—can never be thanked adequately. Others include Dr. Bill Rader, Dr. Nathan Adler, Dr. Harold Demone, Richard Zylman, Dr. John Lee, Dr. Rex Weideranders, Dr. Essie Lee, as well as Helane Anderson and Bob Barnecut of the Marin County Alcohol Information Committee, Aileen Koahn of the Marin N.C.A., Jack Smith, Bob Burger, Herman Menkes and Bob Hutchins of the *AA World News*, Don Sherwood, San Francisco radio personality, and Helen Benson, Carrie Sheriff, Judi McIndoe, and Walter Murphy.

Some of the organizations around the country who helped us in our search for information were the Addiction Research Foundation of Toronto, *The Alcoholism Digest,* Addiction Services Agency of New York, The National Institute on Drug Abuse, General Service Board of Alcoholics Anonymous, Inc., The United States Jaycees and their ambitious Operation THRESHOLD, The Christopher D. Smithers Foundation, Inc., The Addiction Center of Racine, Wisconsin, Rutgers University Center of Alcohol Studies, the Classified Abstract Archives of the Alcohol Literature at Rutgers, the National Clearinghouse for Alcohol Information, Distilled Spirits Council of the United States, Inc., Value Education Publications, and such groups as the Marin Youth Advocates.

Our teen survey was aided by the directors of various institutions: Ronald C. Force of The St. Francis Boys' Homes, Rev. David A. Works of the North Conway Institute, and the coordinators of the Lord Fairfax Health District, The Al-

Acknowledgements

coholism Treatment Center of Danville, Virginia, and the Arlington County Community Alcohol Center in Virginia.

And finally, our thanks to Senator Arlen Gregorio of California and his staff for the wealth of information they provided, and to the staffs in the various Departments of Health in Florida, Georgia, Idaho, Illinois, Massachusetts, Michigan, New Jersey, New Mexico, New York, Pennsylvania, Rhode Island, South Dakota, and Virginia.

Authors' Note

This book is not a sermon against drinking. You'll read no Carry Nation diatribes about Demon Rum. We are not members of rehabilitation or reform organizations or agencies and we have nothing against drinking, per se. We have many friends who drink, our families drink, and we drink ourselves—yes, sometimes too much. We know that there is hardly a parent in the nation—or a teen-ager, for that matter—who hasn't heard ad nauseam about the consequences of immoderate drinking of alcoholic beverages and the pitiful stories of the ultimate effect the alcoholic has on his own life and the lives of those around him. We believe that all the sermons in the world, all the desk-pounding, seminar-studying, and headline-shouting in the world, are not going to change the fact that man has been using excessive amounts of alcohol to alter his reality ever since the Babylonians and Egyptians built the first breweries more than 3,000 years ago.

We're not preaching against drinking. Instead, as parents of daughters aged 12 and 13, we've been tuning in lately to what's going on in the teen world, and we think we have something urgent to tell you. We meet a lot of parents who fall into the "Thank God he's not on drugs" category, which came up again and again in our research, and there's something we want to explain. Alcohol *is* a drug, and incontrovertible evidence shows that it's now the number-one drug choice of teen-age America. Perhaps it's time we admitted to ourselves that our kids may, in fact, be addicted to the most insidious drug of all. Insidious because it's not only *legal,* but because as one psychiatrist put it, "Alcohol first giveth, then it taketh away." It's a lethal and sneaky drug, another told us, because without much warning your teen-ager can overdose on it just as if a junkie were forcing a grimy needle into his innocent young veins.

Second, we feel it's time for some plain talk about the teen-age problem drinker among adults who are mature enough at least to read something about it. No treatises, no doctoral theses, no special jargon or polysyllabic psychiatric terms and phrases to explain some vague esoteric theories and concepts. Just a straight report of what we've found over several months of serious research.

It's time to change the film in our mental movie projectors. The alcoholic of today is *not* Ray Milland seeing bats kill mice on the flophouse wall in *The Lost Weekend*. He is *not* Jack Lemmon groveling like an animal through $10,000 worth of rare plants in his father-in-law's greenhouse to find a pint of gin he hid there two nights ago in *Days of Wine and Roses*. He is *not* the skid row bum sleeping in the doorway, using yesterday's newspaper as a blanket and a candy wrapper as a handkerchief. And, he is *not* the leering, lecherous, party-going harlequin with the lampshade on his head.

Today's alcoholic has become as sophisticated as our society itself. For many years he may be the proverbial pillar of the community. A 30-year-old bank vice-president on the way up. The 50-year-old pastor of your church. Your child's 21-year-old kindergarten teacher. Your best friend, who never drinks more than two sherries. Your cousin, your mother, your partner, your teammate, your lover, your neighborhood policeman. Or even your child. Because psychiatrists will tell you that today's alcoholic, through some phenomenon of conditioning, can often walk without wobbling, drive without weaving, talk without slurring, and work without *obvious* fault.

So it no longer matters that you've never "seen" your daughter drinking. It no longer matters that your son "has never missed a day" at school. What matters is that your daughter in 1976 can be drunk four times a week without your finding out about it for a long time. What matters is that in 1976 your son can have been on the verge of losing his part-time job due to drinking for the past two years without your ever having known about it.

Authors' Note

About 50 young Americans will be killed today and 250 maimed or disfigured because of their drinking or that of friends close to them. About 50 will die in traffic accidents, and half of them because someone was drunk—very often a teen-ager. Statistics abound, and you'll find many of them in the first portion of this book. We have tried to present as faithfully as possible an accurate picture of what's going on in America today as far as teen-age drinking is concerned, and have tried to put forth a representative cross-section of what the newspapers of America are reporting to us. Researchers are soon bombarded with shocking stories and reports from all over the nation, and it is our intent to pass along that same feeling of overwhelming revelation to parents, hence our "shotgunning" of statistics and surveys from all over America. But it seems even these statistics aren't enough. Many people believe what they want to believe, and, in the words of Dr. Morris Chafetz, a psychiatrist and Director of the National Institute on Alcohol Abuse and Alcoholism, "The state of the art of alcohol research today is such that I can produce for you a study that will confirm anything you want to believe."

When we contacted the Distilled Spirits Council of the United States, Inc., (DISCUS) in Washington, D.C. (which uses an Olympian discus thrower as its logo), about getting information on teen-age drinking in America, they reported "scant evidence, if any, to support claims that teen-age alcoholism is on the rise," while virtually every official agency, private research organization, statewide study and county survey in the country was telling us that teen-age problem drinking was on the rise. The words "any" and "claims" bothered us, but we went through an article enclosed in the same envelope. It was a clipping from *Newsday,* December 11, 1973, entitled "Teenage Drinking: On the Increase or Not?" The article was a commendable attempt at objectivity, yet it was decidedly designed to reassure readers about the flood of statistics and surveys indicating an increase in teen-age drinking. The article pointed out that many observers—chiefly a group at Rutgers University—take issue with the validity of the statistics and question the inconsistent weights given various portions of researchers' questions. It said, in part: "Long Island police, for example, report no significant increase in traffic arrests related to alcohol—and school administrators see no marked increase in the dropout rate or in alcohol-related behavior during school hours."

Yet exactly one year later, on December 31, 1974, *Newsday* published an article titled "Teenage Drinking Brings L.I. Response," which deplored the increasing use of alcohol on the part of Long Island's teen-agers and offered specific examples. The article said, "Sparked by reports that a large and growing number of teenagers have drinking problems, a variety of Long Island agencies have started programs to deal with the alcohol problems of the young."

What a difference a year makes. But what really matters, what this book is all about, is that in 1867 in New York City, 3,658 boys and girls between 10 and 15 were arrested for drunkenness, and that the number has been growing during the 106 years since then. In that same year, in fact, a 15-year-old boy was committed to the state institution as a "confirmed drunk" and his 13-year-old brother killed himself in a state of alcoholic depression.

That's the way it was in 1867. Now it's much worse, and instead of wringing our hands and crying "Where did we go wrong?" we're shrugging it off with a sheepish grin and saying "That's my boy!" or, worse, "Thank God he's not on drugs."

Edmond G. Addeo
Jovita Reichling Addeo
Mill Valley, California

Contents

WHY OUR CHILDREN DRINK

PART ONE

ARE TEEN-AGERS DRINKING?

There are two things that will be believed of any man whatsoever, and one of them is that he has taken to drink.

—Booth Tarkington, PENROD

1

The Scope of
the Problem

Back in 1966 in a fashionable New York City suburb, Mike and Sheila T. gave their daughter, Amy, 5, a sip of beer during the course of a casual evening with several friends. Little Amy, cute as a bug, was the oldest child of the social circle and, as such, was the toast of the party. Amy tasted everyone's beer that night, and just before her bedtime, someone noticed she was wobbling erratically, almost comically. Finally she fell to the carpet in a fit of giggles. Everyone laughed as Daddy stood her up again, and Amy twirled across the living room and collapsed once more, this time rolling back again in a fit of laughter. "I think she's smashed," someone observed, to the merriment of the rest.

"She's been mooching sips of beer and I think she's drunk," Mommy said, her brow furrowing. "I don't think that's good for her."

"She'll be fine," Daddy said. "Let's put her to bed and she'll be fine." Everyone laughed again as Amy giggled away and tried to sing one of her kindergarten songs. Wasn't that the cutest thing!

Well, Daddy was wrong and Mommy was right. It wasn't good for her. Eight years later, in 1974, beautiful little Amy, now 13, was a confirmed alcoholic. She had already *traded her body* to an 18-year-old college freshman for two bottles of vodka. She had shoplifted booze from at least three neighborhood liquor stores (caught once), been suspended from school twice for cutting classes, involved in a car collision after a wild drinking party, and had been an alcoholic in every sense of the word since she was 11. Her parents hadn't the vaguest idea she ever drank anything stronger than a sip of Daddy's wine or maybe splitting a beer with Mommy while they washed the family cars on a hot Saturday afternoon. Amy is now a member of Alcoholics Anonymous and has been sober for almost a year.

In 1970 in one of the three largest California cities, young Sal, 12, who had been sneaking "sips" of his father's beer, was caught by a teacher in school as he tried to conceal a Thermos full of vodka and black cherry soda in his locker. The teacher reprimanded him, alerted his parents, and during the subsequent meeting it was decided that "boys will be boys" and that Sal wouldn't do it anymore. Two years later he vomited blood in the middle of the night, was hospitalized and treated for gastritis, and released, apparently recovered. A few months later he came home from a party dead drunk and his parents had a terrible fight with their good friends, the parents of the host youth. They haven't spoken to one another since, and after Sal was discovered last June at the age of 16 having screaming fits in an alcoholic stupor, he was hospitalized. He still hasn't been released.

Bill, now 21, is reported in the *New York Post* as a New

York neighborhood kid who started drinking when he was 11 or 12 years old. The "bunch of guys" used to chip in for a quart of beer, and in order to get even higher than the beer would afford, Bill and his buddies put ashes in the beer and let the beer warm up before drinking it. Later on, after graduating to second and third quarts, then wine and hard liquor, the group finally got older kids to buy booze for them with their lunch money or money stolen either from small merchants or their families. Then they would start cutting classes in the afternoon, because they would get so high at lunchtime they didn't want to come down. "I used to like the head," the *Post* reports Bill as saying. "I wanted to get high, party and goof off. I didn't drink to forget or escape."

But Bill doesn't drink much any more, only a few beers, maybe, when he blows some grass. "I couldn't hack the hard liquor," he told the newspaper. "I would get headaches and throw up. I'd get into arguments and get violent." Bill now feels he can handle alcohol intelligently.

And then there was V., a pretty, doe-eyed 20-year-old who had been drinking since she was 11. She used to get the money by lying to her mother about needing it for some school expense. "To this day I still drink a lot," V. says. "I could drink a fifth right now and be ready for more."

And J., another kid, now 18, says he doesn't drink any more because he gets sick and starts throwing up. But for *four or five years* he was a daily drinker without his parents knowing about it. "I used to like drinking and going to junior high," J. boasts. "Mess around like crazy, fool around with the teachers and get 'em mad. They never knew. I used to stuff a whole pack of gum in my mouth."

Rose joined A.A. at the age of 16, too. A boyfriend got her drunk on beer when she was 13. A bit shy, wanting to be "one of the crowd" she thought she'd learn to "hold her liquor'' so they couldn't make fun of her when she passed out or threw up. She practiced to be the way other people were. She sat in the kitchen at parties and told the dirtiest jokes and drank the most beer. Finally, she was drinking wine and rum. She used to carry an extra-large straw purse so she could easily hide four quarts of whiskey in it. One night when she was 15, someone dropped some LSD into her drink. She snapped and had flashbacks for several months. The state hospital wouldn't take her because of her age. Finally she went to a motel with nine friends and snapped for the last time. She woke up in a hospital, and eventually found her way to A.A. and recovery. Now, at 17, she's back in school, and trying to rebuild her life.

Do you, as a parent, find these stories shocking? Do you think they are only isolated, ''special'' cases that crusading teetotalers and reformed drunks write about in women's magazines? Well, they *are* shocking. But they're shocking not so much for the pitiful condition of each of the kids involved, they're shocking because they are not only absolutely true, but also only a handful of more than a *half million* similar stories of teens and subteens who are hopeless alcoholics in grave danger of killing themselves and their friends. And these are just the *known* underage alcoholics. Virtually every expert and analyst in the country agrees that there are probably more than *two million* preteen, teen-age and ''young adult'' (20-24) problem drinkers or pronounced alcoholics, and the evidence seems to indicate that the figure is rising at nearly an epidemic rate.

Three years ago in Los Angeles, the local A.A. organization had only one chapter for the ''underage'' drinker. Today there are some twenty-five, and the number is increasing. (A.A. does not actually have special ''youth'' chapters; however, more and more chapters are increasingly populated by ''young'' people, who quite naturally gravitate toward other young people's meetings, until chapters emerge where virtually all regular participants are in the same age group.) Fifteen of the chapters have been formed in the past year and a half. "We're the largest teenage drinking problem area in the country, the largest youth-oriented A.A. group in the country, and the fastest-growing youth-drinking area in the country," reports Art Cole, Public Information Director for the Los Angeles Alcoholics Anonymous Central Service Committee. Teen-age alcoholics are estimated at 7,500 in the L.A. area alone.

"The streets of the nation's suburbs are becoming filled with staggering teen-agers and young adults," says one official of the California Department of Mental Health. "It's cheaper to buy a bottle of Ripple than to shell out twenty dollars for a half-lid of decent grass, and the high is just as real. Trouble is, the kids are discovering this by the thousands—the hundreds of thousands, even—and they mistakenly think it's not dangerous because they see their parents drinking all the time."

Moreover, Federal Bureau of Investigation reports state that arrests of youngsters under the age of 18 for driving while drunk have more than doubled in ten years. Social agencies in the San Francisco Bay Area, agreeing that the drop in legal drinking age in most states has spawned the teen-age alcoholism epidemic, say that alcohol in that area has surpassed other drugs as the chief juvenile problem today.

According to Dr. George Outland, Director of Research for California's San Mateo High School District (one of the distressingly few districts around the nation making concerted studies of teen-age drinking problems for the purpose of defining an accurate statistical base for future study), the instance of social alcoholism in high schools is doubling *every two years*.

In Massachusetts, the State Department of Mental Health surveyed high schools in that state and found that 92.7 percent admitted they "use" alcohol and a whopping 59.4 percent admit they get drunk regularly. A survey taken in Maryland showed recently that 69 percent of the ninth-grade students had tried getting high on booze and 84 percent of the eleventh grade had also.

"Grade-school children have been reported coming to school drunk in several areas of this state," reports Wendell Turner, coordinator of the alcoholism programs for Maryland's Prince George's County. "And it's apparent that kids today are drinking specifically to get high, not just to be 'grown up' or 'smart,' as we did in my day."

Joel Bennett, president of the New York Council on Alcoholism estimates that 60 percent of 1,048,000 New York City youngsters between 12 and 18 years of age use alcohol, and that about 36,000 adolescents now show early symptoms of alcoholism and so-called alcohol abuse, according to a report in the *Schenectady Gazette*.

That alcohol is becoming—if it hasn't already become —the principal drug of choice for the nation's teen-agers is corroborated by wide-ranging talks and interviews with the teen-agers themselves. In Chapter 3, we will explore the survey we made of teenage groups around the country, but even a cursory review of published reports in the nation's press indicates that no' one perceives the problem as acutely as the teen-agers themselves.

An official in the San Mateo, California, office of the National Council on Alcoholism said last year, "Everything we have seen leads us to believe kids are starting to use alcohol more, and at an earlier age. Now it's starting from junior high on up." A mother active in San Francisco neighborhood youth programs states what seems to be the prevailing opinion in Northern California; "I just have to talk to my teen-age daughter to know what's going on . . . to know that the problem's getting serious. It's getting out of hand." And a high school counselor in San Francisco told us he deals regularly with 20 problem drinkers among his students. "And it's getting higher every day," he states.

Perhaps one of the leading figures in the field of alcoholism research, especially as pertains to the rise in teen-age drinking, is Morris E. Chafetz, M.D., director of the National Institute on Alcohol Abuse and Alcoholism in Washington, D.C., operating under the auspices of the Department of Health, Education and Welfare. According to Dr. Chafetz, cases of alcoholism among young people, even children between 9 and 12 years old, have increased *tenfold* in the past four years. Chafetz warns that before parents begin relaxing over statistics which show the decline in the use of so-called "hard" drugs, they look at their replacement: alcohol.

"Every indicator and every statistic we have tells us the switch is on," Dr. Chafetz recently told an Oklahoma convention. He emphasized that parental tolerance toward the use of alcohol reflects "an extreme lack of awareness" about the dangers of alcohol abuse to their youngsters. "You must accept the fact that [alcohol] is the most common drug man has historically taken to alter his reality from time to time. You must be familiar with what alcohol does to one's system and to one's mind," he urged parents.

Dr. Chafetz agrees that it's much easier to get parents and educators and P.T.A. groups fired up about the use of drugs because very few of the parents and educators and P.T.A. groups are drug users. "But try to get parents excited about a beverage they've used themselves, and that's a different matter," Dr. Chafetz says. He tells parents that recent studies have shown that approximately 14 percent of all high school senior males say they get drunk at least once a week, and 36 percent say they get drunk at least four times a year.

As parents, let's think about that for a minute. Fourteen percent get drunk *at least* once a week. Now, if 14 percent is, say, one out of seven high school senior males, that means that the average high school senior class has from 10 to 15 kids that are drunk *at least* once a week. Perhaps two or three times, for some; maybe five or six for others. If your son or daughter has, say, ten "close" friends in his or her high school senior class, isn't it worth finding out more about the situation?

Even though the isolated cases that make the headlines are just that, one has only to survey a typical month's output of small town and metropolitan newspapers to see that the problem of increasing teen-age drinking is almost epidemic. At the same time a 17-year-old girl was found driving along the runway of San Francisco International Airport in the early hours of a weekday morning and "too drunk to stand or answer questions." The Newark *Star-Ledger* is reporting the arrest of an 18-year-old Philadelphia "man" who survived a car crash while drunk and in which four teen-age companions were killed, and a small-town Wisconsin paper reports that police are investigating the case of a 13-year-old boy found so drunk he "had to be hospitalized." In Fort Worth, at a public hearing on alcoholism, Sara Whitley, executive director of the Dallas Council on Alcoholism, stated that alcohol abusers "showing up among the very young" is a great problem of the day, and that "We find . . . teens in high school, junior high, and even elementary school pupils who have [their own] problems with alcohol." On the same day, an Omaha newspaper reports that the Nebraska Department of Roads is alarmed at the "frightening" increase in alcohol-related traffic deaths among teenagers. That evening a Scranton newspaper reports the arrest of a man who rented a motel room to serve alcoholic beverages to teen-agers and was found out because dozens and dozens of teen-agers were seen entering the room. Incidentally, he was released on $500 bail. Headlines in Boston and Biloxi, Salem and San Diego, Fargo and Fort Lauderdale scream the same appalling warning: Alcohol is not only the number-one drug problem among teen-agers today, it is also increasing rapidly as each new survey is taken.

One of the most comprehensive and important studies ever done (and extensively reported in the nation's newspapers) on the subject of teen-age drinking changes was—and is still being—conducted by the Addiction Research Foundation in Toronto, Ontario, Canada. We say "one of the most comprehensive" because one of the disturbing statistics about the teen-age drinking problem in North America today is the lack of research. There have been *only* two long-term, *continuing* studies conducted in the English language. One was in Canada; the other was conducted by the San Mateo County Department of Public Health in Northern California.

The Toronto study, published by Dr. Reginald G. Smart and Diane Fejer, states:

> The authors have been unable to find more than one long-term study of drug use in English. (A footnote explains that one has been conducted in Norway and its English translation is in progress as of early 1975.) The only other study following drug use in a particular area over an extended period of time has been conducted by [the San Mateo group]. Annual studies were conducted among high school students in San Mateo County from 1968 to 1974. As in the Toronto study, the use of many drugs (i.e. alcohol, amphetamines, barbiturates, marijuana, and LSD) increased substantially between 1968 and 1971; then the rate of increase tended to slow down or stabilize. The 1974 data from this study indicated that the use of very few drugs had increased over the past year; definite declines were found in the use of barbiturates and tobacco. *Alcohol use continued to increase in San Mateo County as it had from 1968* (our emphasis). Since so few long-term trend studies are available it is of

interest to compare the data from the Toronto studies with that of San Mateo County.

The report goes on to explain how the results of the two studies show the same significant increase in teen-age drinking over the same six-year period. It concluded that:

> Probably the most notable change which occurred during the past two years involved the use of alcohol. Alcohol use increased by about 10 percent during this period. So about 71 percent of the students in Grades 7, 9, 11 and 13 presently drink at least once a month. (For a more detailed discussion of this report, see Appendix.)

The San Mateo County report, which is the *only* other long-term study conducted in the English language, was markedly similar to the Toronto report. The survey was designed and conducted by the Research and Statistics Section of the San Mateo County Department of Public Health and Welfare. All public high school districts in the county except one participated, including all parochial and private schools, again with the exception of one. The 1968 survey included the responses of 18,774 high school students; the 1969 survey included 23,649 responses.

The survey asked students about their use of five ''mind-altering'' substances: alcoholic beverages, tobacco, marijuana, LSD, and amphetamines within the twelve months preceding the survey. The alcohol portion of the San Mateo study results stated:

> Our data indicate that the use of alcoholic beverages is *not only widespread but also increased both in extent and intensity* . . . rates for alcohol usage increased sharply with grade [and] rates for girls were surprisingly close to

boys, but lower in the ten times or more use category.
(our emphasis)

Nancy Gilbert, writing for the Youth Service wire, reported a survey of 484 high school and college students throughout the United States and discovered that more than half of them "drank alcohol." The service reported that 50 percent said they found many young people of their acquaintance were getting drunk at least once a week. Parties seemed to be the major place where the drinking occurred, with parked cars, dances, and drive-in movies following in that order. Nine percent reported they drank "quite often," 27 percent "never," and 29 percent "sometimes." The explanations students offered as to the popularity of alcohol were reported thus:

—Because it's illegal and they do it to look older!"

—"It's something to do, especially around here. There's nothing to do on weekends."

—"Drugs are too expensive and some of them are dangerous."

—"It's a good way out of all the pressures parents and school put on kids."

—"They like it better than drugs. Besides, it's something their parents do."

—"No guilt feelings involved, like when you're smoking pot."

—"It's a fad, like drugs. They want something to do that will make them seem cool."

And this is Americas' next generation!

In Connecticut, *The Hartford Times* quoted Dr. Norman Wolfish, of the Children's Hospital of Eastern Ontario in Ottawa, as saying that more than *one* percent of all 16-year-olds in the United States and Canada are "desperate, chronic alcoholics." Dr. Wolfish continued, "Young persons have turned to the old, reliable, easily obtainable and socially acceptable panacea of all ills—alcohol."

In upstate New York, several news reports in the beginning of 1975 warned that teen-age drinking was increasing, and, in fact, the Broome County Alcoholism Center at the Binghamton General Hospital reported that the number of teen-agers treated had more than tripled from last year to this.

In an "Alcohol Awareness Week" session in Massachusetts (where the rate of alcoholism is fourth largest in the country behind California, New York, and Rhode Island), it was pointed out that while there are 300,000 heroin users in the entire nation, there are almost as many persons (299,000) "in trouble with alcohol" *in Massachusetts alone*, and there is general agreement among state officials that the highest rate of increase in alcohol abuse is among persons under 21 years of age. In a letter to the *Boston Globe*, James P. Richards, executive director of the Mount Pleasant Hospital in Lynn, Massachusetts, states: "Teenage abuse of alcohol is a glaring reality in our Massachusetts communities," and that while the documented facts on the cases that get to the courts are shocking, the number of teen-age alcoholic cases which are kept under wraps "under the guise of protecting juveniles" is downright appalling.

"This hospital has handled dozens of young people who get to us after the diagnosis of acute or chronic alcoholism," Richards states. "These are people 16, 17 and 18 years old. Can we stop deceiving ourselves that enough is being done in the home, the schools, the churches, or the community at large?"

In Chicago, school authorities and social advisers agree that teen-age drinking is definitely on the rise, and that the kids are "middle-class whites," rather than minorities. "They're definitely not what you'd call the schools 'hundred worst' or anything like that,'' states Dr. Edward Kealy, research director of Alternatives. Dr. Kealy said "recreational drinking"—as opposed to "problem drinking"—is engaged in by 10 or 20 percent of elementary school children as well as high school students.

"Approximately 40 percent of the kids we see who are 16 or older are strung out on alcohol at least during the weekend, and many of them once a day,'' reports John Katonah, program director of the North River Youth Services Project. At a teen center called Canterbury House, a staff member concurs that there is "a definite shift" toward alcohol as the preferred drug on which to get high, and in a newspaper survey of surrounding school districts the consensus among teachers and administrators is nearly unanimous that alcohol abuse is on the rise. "Teens seem to prefer whatever is the cheapest,'' one official said, citing "the kind of wine you can buy for two dollars a gallon and still have change.''

However, Dr. Phyllis Snyder, director of Chicago's Alcoholic Treatment Center, doubts there is any "epidemic" in teen-age drinking. As reported in the *Chicago Sun-Times*, Dr. Snyder said, "I don't think the prevalence of kids using alcohol today is much greater than it was long ago. Kids drank then. Kids drink now. The only difference is that today kids are more open about it.''

School officials in the Chicago area, though, seem somewhat alarmed. One English teacher said, "It's not unusual for kids to show up at seven-thirty in the morning already drunk.'' Cook County Schools Superintendent Richard J. Martwick believes that the lowering of the drinking age to 19 is one of the factors of seemingly increased teen-age drinking. "It's like a cancer,'' he says. "It catches on. I wonder whether we've used good judgment.''

In Colorado, whose Department of Health officials greet

requests for information about teen-age drinking with "Unfortunately, we have no information on this subject at this time," an informal survey of health officials reveals that the state is somewhat typical in its awareness of the use of alcohol by young people. One counselor has been reported as saying, "It's so obvious that alcohol is our greatest drug problem in the schools," and another with "Alcohol has always been so high [in popularity] that the other drugs never came close." In one Colorado county school system, a survey found that more than 80 percent of school children have tried some form of alcohol by the time they reach the fifth grade, and that in the high schools more than *90* percent of students would be described as "regular users" of alcohol.

While the Colorado Department of Health had "no information," the Department of Education found in early 1975 that out of 126 Colorado school districts, more than 75 percent report they have some kind of alcohol abuse problems in their schools. One official hinted off the record that "some parents are encouraging their kids to drink," apparently thinking it would reduce their desire for other drugs.

The *Rocky Mountain News* in Denver reported recently, "All available data indicate that alcohol use is great and growing among young people in Colorado. Some will live comfortably with their drinking. Others will die from it."

The *Los Angeles Times* recently reported a "birthday" celebrated in a San Fernando Valley chapter of A.A. by an 11-year-old kid. He had been a member for a whole year. At the same meeting, another member told how glad he was that he had stuck it out for a whole month at the A.A. meetings. He was only 10. Both of them were part of a growing number of *very* young alcoholics in the area—subteen and teen-agers estimated to be about 7,500 in the L.A. area alone!

Los Angeles seems to be the nation's hotbed of teen-age

drinking and alcoholism, according to most reports. Art Cole of the L.A. Central Service Committee of Alcoholics Anonymous, in a letter to Dr. E. Farley Hunter of the Office of Alcohol Abuse and Alcoholism of the L.A. County Department of Health Services, stated: "We have at least 100 members of Alcoholics Anonymous in the County who are under 18 years of age, and members as young as 11 and 12 years old. Many of our members under 21 have been active in the fellowship for two, three, and four years. Cole continued: "I do not know of any other resources of primary help for teenage drinking problems within L.A. County at this time." He told us that Los Angeles has been acknowledged as the largest segment of teen-age alcoholics in a single city in the United States, the largest youth-active A.A. chapter in the world, and as a general area, the fastest-growing teen-age drinking problem setting in the nation. Cole gets calls monthly from as far away as Nicaragua and London, and on a more frequent basis, from other chapters of A.A. around the nation with little experience in handling youngsters who at last have recognized their problem and want to join.

Cole said, "The tendency is for an older member to think, 'Hey, I've spilled more booze than you could ever drink kid—how come you're here?' The idea is that the kid's age doesn't disqualify him from being an alcoholic. We're finding out a lot about the kids just by being here in Los Angeles and having our doors open."

The *Times* also reported on the switch ". . .from Dope to Drink" in an article which surveyed college people in Los Angeles County. The college kids still have beer busts, reported *Times* writer Betty Liddick, but now they also enjoy daiquiris flavored with bananas or strawberries on the warm spring nights. Zeta Beta Tau fraternity boys at U.C.L.A. keep blenders in their rooms. The editor of the U.S.C. *Trojan* says

17

they still smoke dope, but now they have parties where they stipulate "Bring Your Own Booze," much like their suburban sophisticate counterparts.

Ms. Liddick emphasized "What *is* startling, however, is the latest word from administrators, advisers, alcoholism experts, and the students themselves that campus drinking has grown *harder, heavier and more frequent.*" (Our emphasis)

One "longtime advisor" to a U.C.L.A. student group commented about an end-of-semester party, according to the article, "I never saw anything like this year. They were drinking like there was no tomorrow."

Campus drinking has been with us since the first college, but the innocent beers at the tables down at Mory's, the pony keg in the frat house during the monthly poker game, the chug-a-lugging over pizzas after the homecoming game are no more. Of the 23,000 students of the University of Massachusetts campus at Amherst, 10 percent are considered problem drinkers—potential alcoholics. A student at a large Midwestern university says, "Drinking is definitely the 'in' thing. On weekends, there's a veritable exodus over the Michigan border, where the age limit is 18 and the campus is loaded with dozens of [booze] parties..." A coed at an Eastern university says, "Drinking is definitely part of college life. We had a blast one night when someone brought a keg of beer into the shower room of a coed dorm. It was wild."

In Glendale, California, the coordinator of physical education for the school district, Al Forthman, pinpoints parental attitudes as a contributory factor toward increased teen-age drinking. "I think we've left the drug trend and are now in a drinking trend," he said recently. "According to parents, this seems to be an acceptable social fact. Parents are giving a big sigh of relief now that the drug problem is dying down and the kids are into beer and wine." Mr. Forthman adds that the proliferation of cheap wines ("Colorado Kool-Aid") is another reason. "Kids are drinking beer and wine simply because they cost less than hard liquor and are considered less dangerous than either drugs or hard liquor."

"Teen-agers can throw it off pretty well," reports Mrs. Narcy Ainsworth, an alcoholism counselor for the Glendale Adventist Medical Center. "Teen-agers are cynical and say, 'It can't happen to me.' Older people seem to drink more because of loneliness. With younger people, it's restlessness and boredom." The youngest alcoholic she has personally encountered was 13. A survey of the students at Hoover High School found that a lot of drinking takes place on weekends, especially after football games. One student answered, "During the football season, the whole school could get arrested." The Glendale Police Department confirmed that 100 juveniles were arrested for liquor law violations in 1973, double the number the previous year. Captain Bob Buehner of the Juvenile Bureau, told a local newspaper that for every incident that comes to police attention, "probably 400 or 500 don't."

The principal of Millbrook Senior High School in a suburb of Raleigh, North Carolina, recently said that in 1974 no students in his high school were sent home for illegal drugs, but that a number had been "carried home" for drinking wine, beer, or whiskey. Delma C. Blinson, principal of nearby Garner Senior High agrees: "The most prominent [drug] use is alcohol. We have noticed an alarming increase in its use." She told a local newspaper that she had sent home 12 kids in one semester because they were drunk or sick from alcohol abuse, whereas the school had only 2 or 3 cases in a similar period the previous year.

In Greensboro, North Carolina, an organization called Switchboard works with young drug users and takes calls for advice and guidance. The Greensboro police department reports that 289 youngsters under 18 were arrested for public drunkenness in 1972, 1973, and 1974, while in 1962, 1963, and 1964 there were only 95. Switchboard director Tony Speed said recently, "There is definitely an increase in the amount of drinking among young people. I think more are turning to alcohol for their highs because it's safer. You can't get busted as easily." A survey made in Greensboro two years ago by CARES, an educational arm of the local alcoholic beverage control board, found that 50 percent of seniors in four regional high schools said they had downed their first real drink before they reached the ninth grade and *one-third* said they were now regular drinkers. And, for those arguing the validity of alcohol as a toxic drug, Dr. Page Hudson of Chapel Hill, the state medical examiner, said that alcohol causes 30 times more deaths in North Carolina than all other drugs combined.

Clear across the country in Tacoma, Washington, Jean Hibbard, coordinator of the poison center at Mary Bridge Children's Health Center said that 2-year-old children have been brought into the center because of an overdose of alcohol. "But they get drunk by accident in the home," she reported. "Teen-agers do it on purpose, and the trend among these young people has moved from drugs to alcohol." She added that there is "a growing number" of teen-age alcoholics, "young people actually afflicted with the disease of alcoholism."

In Poughkeepsie, New York, an alcoholism expert, a police criminal investigator, and the director of the Dutchess County Youthful Drug Abuse program all agree that a "stepped-up" use of alcohol is becoming evident since New York State changed its drug laws in 1974. "Just after the drug laws were changed, we began hearing that drinking had increased," said Patricia Mitchell, of the federally funded Alcoholism Information Center. Captain Joseph Leary, chief of the Bureau of Criminal Investigation for Troop K of the State Police, added, "There is a growing feeling that 'kids' might as well drink because they can't get busted for carrying booze. They figure they can get whatever they're looking for with alcohol without the fear of being arrested for possession. [Drinking] is definitely increasing and we have come across it much more frequently in the past year.'' Dennis Pearl, director of the youth program, concurs and adds that in his personal experience he has seen ''a greater use of alcohol in the past year among county youngsters.''

In an interview with a local newspaper, Ms. Mitchell spoke of a junior high school student who expressed concern about the number of eighth-graders who were drinking, and of a fifth-grade boy who asked her whether he was an alcoholic because he was drinking a can of beer *a day*. That's the fifth grade—can you imagine your own fifth-grader drinking a can of beer a day? Probably not, and it's precisely this inability to translate certain drinking behavior to their own children that blinds most parents to a problem which may be developing in their own home. One friend of ours scoffed when we discussed this particular fifth-grader recently, saying that any parent who couldn't at least *smell* beer every day—for heaven's sake!—didn't deserve to be a parent. We agreed. Then we asked her own fifth-grader whether she knew of any kids who drank beer. The child became fearful and admitted that one particular kid in the class bragged about smuggling beer from the family refrigerator when he got home from school every day (both parents worked) and simply brushed his teeth ''real hard'' just before dinnertime. Now, even though our friend was surprised that such a thing could be happening, and at the same time believed that it wasn't one of her kid's close friends, the point to remember is this: if there is *one* fifth-grader drinking beer on a regular basis without being detected, think of the pressure on your children over the next seven years to take a drink, until at the age of 17 and about to go off to the ''freedom'' of college he will have had, in all probability, a wide

21

range of drinking experiences *without your knowledge*. Wouldn't you agree it was time way back in the fifth grade to start educating yourself *and* your child about alcohol and its implications?

Illinois admits to having 934,000 alcoholics or problem drinkers, of whom 35 percent are in the educational system. *A fantastic 85 percent of that group is between grades 9 and 12!* Specifically, of the 657,726 kids enrolled in grades 9 through 12, according to one statewide report, 279,977 are having varying degrees of difficulty with alcoholic beverages. This is a total of 42.6 percent—*almost half!*—of the kids in the average Illinois high school.

Now, this is alarming enough to parents in Illinois, but what about parents in high teen-age drinking states with large urban areas such as California, New York, Massachusetts, and say, Michigan?

An indicator of youthful drinking is found in a 1971 survey of tenth-, eleventh-, and twelfth-graders at two Warwick, Rhode Island, high schools. A 25 percent cross section (1,000 students) indicated the following:

1. 95.1 percent revealed that they had had *some* experience with beers and wines, with 13.1 percent saying that they drank them "frequently."

2. 83.5 percent revealed they had had *some* experience with hard liquors, with 4.9 percent saying that they used hard liquor "frequently."

There are over 54,000 students in grades 10, 11, and 12 in Rhode Island (approximate age 15 to 18 years old). If Warwick is representative of the rest of the state, about 7,000 teen-agers in these three grades drink beer and wine "frequently" and about 2,500 such teen-agers drink hard liquor "frequently."

A survey of 589 high school students in Washtenaw County, Michigan, showed that 76 percent of those polled had consumed alcohol, as opposed to 66 percent in 1960. The survey found that kids not only drank more, but drank *harder*, too. In 1972, 20 percent said they most frequently downed five or more drinks in one sitting; in 1970, only two years earlier, 12 percent said the same.

In Arizona, a university survey classified 61,200 residents under 24 as heavy problem drinkers. Based on census figures, *one in five* persons between the ages of 13 and 24 in Arizona is an alcoholic!

The Community Services and Environmental Protection Committee of Hartford, Connecticut, met recently to determine what could be done about a problem local residents had been noticing: school yards every Monday morning seemed increasingly to be littered with empty gin and vodka bottles or premixed screwdriver bottles. In wastebaskets in the washrooms of the school, janitors and teachers also were finding empty liquor bottles. Councilwoman Mary Heslin took the time to tell of a 16-year-old freshman who had spent the weekend in Hartford Hospital in convulsions after drinking almost a quart of booze. It was generally agreed by school officials, other councilmen and Judy Wolfson, executive director of the Connecticut State Alcohol Community Planning Organization, that "teen-agers seem to be switching away from hard drug use and toward the substitution of alcohol." Ms. Wolfson even used the term we heard again and again during our research—parents inevitably seem to say, "Thank God it's not drugs" when they find their children are consuming alcoholic beverages.

In Vancouver, two researchers sampled 10 percent of the high school students and are satisfied that their findings apply to all 28,000 students in the area: 71 percent of the students are now using alcohol, compared with 61 percent four years ago.

In "The Young Alcoholics," Los Angeles television station KNXT-TV used a Field Research Corporation survey showing that teen-age drinking is more damaging than drugs and that most parents aren't aware of the extent to which young people drink. Are we too busy drinking ourselves? Can it be that we don't quite realize that a sermon about not smoking marijuana or chug-a-lugging beer doesn't fall upon attentive ears when it's given with a cigarette in one hand and a double martini in the other? The Field survey found that 43 percent of parents really believe their children never drink. Are you one? Of all the parents surveyed, 74 percent of the fathers and 45 percent of the mothers admitted that *they* drank when they were young. What an appalling case of doublethink! There are actually almost half of us who sincerely think our kids don't drink, yet almost three-quarters of the dads and half of the moms drank when they were young.

Although there are few significant teen-age drinking *programs* being carried out on a statewide basis, there have been several random quantitative studies carried out by individual groups and smaller agencies around the nation. Their results are almost unanimous—there *is* a problem. Dr. Glenn D. Mellinger of the Institute for Research in Social Behavior, Berkeley, California, conducted a study of alcohol and drug use on campus by university men ages 17 to 19 in 1970, and a follow-up study two and a half years later. A total of 834 freshmen students were polled. At the beginning of the study, the use of marijuana was marked, but in the follow-up study it became obvious that alcohol had replaced pot as the drug of choice.

—In 1970, 24 percent said they used alcohol one or more times a week; in 1972, the figure was almost double at 44 percent.

—In 1970, 6 percent said they used alcohol three or more times a week; in 1972, the figure was almost *triple* at 17 percent.

The Scope of the Problem

The phrase Dr. Mellinger used in his conclusions was "an alarming trend" toward the increased use of alcohol over the two-and-a-half year period for the same age group.

Even in the distant, relatively calm and tension-free era of the Kennedy administration, when the flower children had not yet invaded San Francisco's Haight-Ashbury, when the drug culture was still that dark and murky nether world of "dope fiends" and Frank Sinatra's writhing in his self-inflicted prison-bedroom was still fresh in our minds, a Nassau County, Long Island study showed that an astronomical 88 percent of kids between 14 and 18 years of age drank "regularly." Of those 16 and older, 90 percent drank; 35 percent said that they had been drunk at least once and 18 percent said they had gotten sick from drinking. Three-fourths of all the kids said their parents allowed them to drink at home, and 50 percent had permission to drink away from home. A similar study on Staten Island showed that 59 percent drank at home.

Again, this was back in 1963.

Even before 1960 the problem was apparent. Dr. Vernelle Fox, Chief of Alcoholism Services of Long Beach General Hospital, California, called teen-age drinking "the bone of contention in the dogfight between the generations." On the trend which started during the '60s as the drug culture subsided, and the cost of pot increased and illegal possesion crackdowns became more intensified, Dr. Fox added, "The current trend in drug use by youth is shifting back toward alcohol as the drug of choice. It appears that we are passing a peak of drug experimentation and are leveling out with a more chronic use pattern of mixed substance abuse, with alcohol quite prominent in the picture."

Often the students or teen-agers themselves comment upon the accuracy of the surveys taken. *Newsday* recently reported a study taken of East Islip (New York) High School juniors which indicated that 28 percent had taken harmful

25

drugs compared with 20 percent a year ago, and that school officials attributed the increase to a pronounced increase in the use of alcohol by the student body. When questioned after school about the results of the survey by the newspaper reporter, a group of students said they thought the survey was quite accurate and, if anything, probably underestimated the prominence of alcohol use by students. One 18-year-old senior said "everybody" drinks; all agreed that peer pressure is the big factor in alcohol abuse. "It's social pressure," one 16-year-old is reported to have said. "Sometimes it's forced on you."

When asked, "How many people do you know your age who drink?" four students in an alcoholic education clinic in Seattle finally ended their haggling and calculating and agreed on the number—3,000. When questioned about the size of this figure, the kids didn't flinch. "Man, everybody drinks at my school," one said. "If not a lot, then a little something on a regular basis."

Even their teachers agree. In Chicago, at a recent workshop conducted by Richard J. Martwick, Cook County Superintendent of Schools, 150 school administrators, deans, nurses, counselors, social workers and school board members found that among junior and seniors in suburban high schools:

—85 (of the 151 educators) indicated they observed an increase in the consumption of alcoholic beverages among their students (56 percent).

—87 currently consider alcohol abuse a more significant health problem than "hard" drugs (59 percent).

—only 50 believed their student counseling programs were effective (33 percent).

Martwick said, "School administrators and personnel are coming to realize the seriousness of student alcoholism. It is up to us to inform all parents as well as [to] educate students of the harmful effects of alcohol and to remove the 'respectable' label from it.''

Even the *bartenders* are corroborating the youth-alcohol trend! Although in states such as California a person must show proof of being 21 years of age to drink legally, experts agree that a young person who frequents bars, saloons, and cocktail lounges almost surely received his early drinking training in high school and college. In an article in the *San Francisco Examiner*, a survey of bartenders showed that ''hundreds of those long-haired young people they used to call hippies are lining up six to eight deep'' at several favorite watering holes along favorite strips.

''Tequila! My God, do I sell a lot of tequila!'' cries one bartender in the article. He explains that the young set no longer opts for the wines and beers of the sixties, but now asks for harder stuff: tequila, vodka, scotch, and gin.

The bartender touched on an interesting point. Tequila is indeed one of the two most popular hard drinks the kids are taking to, the other being vodka. Called the ''whites,'' these liquors are easier to hide, explains Jerry Sanders, volunteer director and a founder of a teen-age alcoholism program in L.A.'s San Fernando Valley. Student drinkers stash the ''whites'' in nail polish remover bottles and milk cartons, he says. Further investigation shows that another reason for vodka's popularity—perhaps the overwhelming reason—is that it's odorless, so that it can be mixed with practically any approved beverage (soda, milk in the school Thermos, ''pop'' wines, etc.) and still not be detected on the drinker's breath when he gets home.

Big Daddy ought to tell us whether the San Francisco bartenders are right. Big Daddy, whose real name is Joseph Flannigan, owns and operates more than seventy-five bars and cocktail lounges in Florida, California and Texas which are frequented for the most part by young people. Big Daddy reports that his business has increased by one-fifth, maybe even one-fourth, since the drinking age was lowered to 18 years old in Florida. Reportedly, his biggest problem now is keeping out underage kids—16- and 17-year-olds, who try to get into his bars with phony ID cards.

It's significant that business has fallen *off* at Big Daddy's chain of package stores. ''I guess the kids don't have to find someone to go in and buy their bottles from my stores when they can just go into my saloons now and drink with their friends,'' he said.

But students, educators, and even bartenders cannot begin to describe the national scope of the rapid rise in teenage drinking. Even municipalities and town councils are beginning to reexamine ordinances to enforce public drinking laws and perhaps cut down the appalling 40 percent of traffic fatalities nationally which are alcohol related. In New Brunswick, New Jersey, the Madison township council had voted to permit Lake Duhernal to be used for parties at night, and under pressure also permitted drinking at the site, even though there is an ordinance prohibiting the use of alcohol at the lake. Within a few months, 50 of the residents nearby threatened to form a vigilante committee unless the authorities took measures to curtail the vandalism, malicious mischief, and destruction of property that suddenly erupted due to the wave of drunken teen-agers that infested the area, almost nightly. Candidly admitting that the experimental program at the lake had backfired, officials introduced new measures in the form of antiloitering and antidrinking ordinances, and the police department was ordered to make patrols of the area in question and of the streets in general after hours.

One evening, 63 juveniles were arrested and charged with illegal possession of alcoholic beverages. One of them was a 12-year-old girl. In the weeks to follow, more arrests were made and finally there were more than 100 charged with various alcohol-oriented offenses.

The Scope of the Problem

Near Hackensack, New Jersey, youthful drinking in the town of Dumont has resulted in the introduction of an ordinance to outlaw drinking or carrying open alcoholic beverages on any public property, including streets. Six other Bergen County communities—Ridgefield Park, Glen Rock, Lodi, North Arlington, Rochelle Park, and Closter—have instituted similar ordinances. In an editorial, *The Record* stated, in part:

> Parents are loath to identify their children as problem drinkers, some parents because they are ashamed, some because they don't recognize the symptoms, many because they prefer—mistakenly—to see their children wrestling with alcohol instead of drugs.

At the Westwood Kiwanis Club, near Johnstown, Pennsylvania, Curt Hamel, the area representative of the National Child Safety Council, told a luncheon meeting that the Vietnam war had opened a pandora's box in transporting hard drugs into the United States. "And the worst of these is alcohol. There are alcoholics as young as 9 years of age." He added that because drugs are expensive, "alcohol has once again become the number-one problem with children."

Early in 1975, *The Hutchinson News* (Kansas) ran a series of articles on adolescent alcoholics, in which the editors prefaced the first installment of the series in this way:

> Editor's Note: Alcohol is the most easily obtained and acceptable social drug in the United States. It is also the most misused drug, researchers believe. Their studies show that alcohol is misused by adults and adolescents alike. Teenagers with alcoholic problems appear to be increasing in numbers, some juvenile authorities warn . . .

The first of the articles, written by reporter Gerald Hay,

29

shows how the majority of "drug addicts" in America today aren't sniffing cocaine, blowing grass, popping pills, or "silently feeding hungry veins with needles." They are pulling pop-top tabs from beer cans or twisting caps from bottles of wine and liquor. The article also quotes Bill Hager, director of the Reno County Alcoholic Treatment Facility: "Teen-age alcoholism is definitely a problem (in Hutchinson, Kansas). It's a bigger problem than anyone realizes, or cares to realize." Hager estimates that 90 percent of the area's high school teenagers have experienced the use of alcohol and that "a third of the students are drinking on a regular basis."

Even P.T.A. groups are acknowledging the drastic increase in teen-age drinking and are spending huge funds to investigate. The National Parent-Teachers Association, acting under a grant of $100,000 from the National Institute on Alcohol Abuse and Alcoholism, has distributed funds to no less than eighteen state P.T.A. groups for the purpose of "finding solutions to the growing problem of alcoholism among young people." These include Arizona, Arkansas, California, Iowa, Michigan, New York, Ohio, South Dakota, Tennessee, Utah and Oregon. The grants seem to range anywhere from $1,900 to $4,125. "Mini-grants" of from $700 to $1,300 have been awarded to six other states. Any reader connected with a P.T.A. organization which feels it has a plan of action for implementing a significant program directed toward teen-age alcoholism is urged to contact the National P.T.A. for information about the grants. Some important and far-reaching discoveries and conclusions may be hiding just under the surface of your own group's activities on the local youth scene.

That the problem is definitely on the rise among teens is overwhelmingly evident. More than ten years ago, New Hampshire—a state not usually associated with heavily drinking teen-agers—studied teen-age drinking habits from a representative sampling of 536 New Hampshire junior-senior high school students. The results showed that "in the breakdown it was considered likely that the decision whether to drink would be influenced by the relative importance, to the student, of conflicting attitudes of 'buddies,' the 'gang,' the opposite sex, parents, and community. The pull and tug of these reference group opinions would be heightened if alcohol produced physiological or behavioral changes in the teenager." The study coined arbitrary "weathervane" labels for such changes, the most significant of which are "pivotal," or "pivotal drinkers," which refer to:

a) getting drunk, sick, arrested, unusual behavior, fighting, passed out, blacking out (not remembering certain times during drinking, although the drinker has not "passed out");
b) drinking alone or whenever a chance occurs; before a party or before breakfast;
c) drinking in cars, bars, alleys; using false proof of age to obtain liquor; drinking when parents are not at home.

The New Hampshire survey revealed a few noteworthy statistics for parents:

1. 26 percent of males and 11 percent of females in the seventh grade DRANK REGULARLY; 21 percent and 12 percent, respectively, in the eighth grade; 40 percent and 26 percent in the ninth grade; 37 percent and 26 percent in the tenth grade; 58 percent and 42 percent in the eleventh grade; and 58 percent and 48 percent in the twelfth grade. (Note the striking similarity of the regular drinkers in the seventh grade to the eighth grade; the ninth grade to the tenth; and the eleventh to the twelfth.)

2. Pivotal drinkers represented a full two-thirds of the "drinkers" in the *seventh* grade. Roughly 20 percent of the

"regular drinkers" in each grade sampled were pivotal drinkers.

3. In the ninth grade, there were more regular female
drinkers than male drinkers.

4. The majority of parents *did not know* of their kids'
drinking in most grades.

5. The 44 high-frequency drinkers and pivotal repeaters
(who drank 41 or more times in six months and had pivotal
reactions six or more times) represented 8 percent of the sample. These students, most of whom were in the twelfth grade,
were dependent upon alcohol in some form of another.

And that study was taken more than ten years ago! The
most recent shocker shows that from that New Hampshire
survey with 8 percent dependent on alcohol in some way,
we've reached as high as 12 percent in some cities. In a study
released on February 19, 1975, a survey of 10,000 juniors
and seniors revealed that more than 15,000 of the 136,000
students in New York's public high schools either may already
be alcoholics or show significant signs of potential alcoholism.
This new study, conducted with questionnaires filled out by
students from 16 to 19 in ninety-one separate schools under the
auspicies of the Department of Mental Health and Mental
Retardation Services, the Board of Education, and Hunter College, showed that 80 percent of the students drank, and a
startling 12 percent drank in classic alcoholic patterns. The
survey pointed out that there was a definite correlation between problem drinking and beginning to drink before the
seventh grade. According to Dr. Gilbert M. Shimmel of
Hunter College, "There is a hard core of problem drinkers (in
public high schools), and the age at which young people begin
to drink is going down."

In a number of surveys conducted early this year in and
near Palo Alto, California, similar results were emphasized by
alarmed teachers. In a report to the City of Palo Alto by the

John F. Kennedy University Institute for Drug Abuse Education and Research, some local fifth-graders (about 10 or 11 years old) were coming to school drunk, with bottles of liquor in their possession. In a survey conducted by the nearby Mountain View Community Health Abuse Council, which utilized questionnaires completed by more than 4,000 seventh- to twelfth-graders in seven different schools, 10.4 percent of the seventh-grade boys had used alcohol more than 50 times in one school year, and 34 percent of the twelfth-graders had. And finally, teachers at Palo Alto's Cubberly High School reported that 75 percent of the students "drank," 42 percent said they'd been drunk "in school," and a surprising 10 percent said they "went to school loaded" almost every day. (Some 61 percent were reported to have been in a classroom where they thought the teacher "appeared intoxicated.")

A Kentucky survey conducted in 1972 by R. L. Kane and E. Patterson found that 3 percent of 21,264 high school students in seven northern Kentucky counties were heavy drinkers (three or more times per week), and 8 percent of those surveyed said they drank every weekend. Considering that the 3 percent was probably part of the 8 percent, that's still almost 2,000 students drinking every weekend or doing some serious drinking at least once a week. What's more, 34 percent reported drinking more than six drinks at a "sitting," indicating once again that kids are not only drinking more, they're drinking harder, too.

Sister Thomasina Reehil, director of the Perth Amboy (New Jersey) General Hospital Escape Center, a drug treatment facility, and Dr. David J. Powell, director of the hospital's alcoholism center, conducted a survey of 935 Middlesex County students between the ages of 14 and 19. Of the 935, *three-fourths* said they had already used alcohol and *one-third* said they used it "frequently, almost daily." Sister

Thomasina reported that her survey revealed that of the drinkers, 50 percent claimed they drank "for pleasure," and the rest drank because of "curiosity, kicks and boredom."

A Pierre, South Dakota, statewide survey last year of "regular drinkers," including some high school surveys on youth drinking, concluded that "more than 9 percent of the state's regular drinkers are either in high school or of high school age." This tends to bear out the statement of Dr. Morris Chafetz that in the government's now-famous Second Special Report on Alcohol and Health, the figure of 5 percent of the nation's teen-agers and subteens as problem drinkers is low. Dr. Chafetz said in an interview that the teen-agers themselves reported to researchers that the figure "should be more like 20 percent." In the South Dakota survey, the 9 percent was something of a surprise because of the state's relatively low density and generally "rural" nature, but it isn't a surprise to anyone who has researched teen-age drinking habits for any length of time.

The Pierre survey, published in *The Brewery*, the monthly magazine of the Division of Alcoholism in Pierre, found that at two separate high schools which were surveyed by their respective journalism classes, 78 percent of senior males and 68 percent of females drink once a week or more, as do 69 percent of junior males and 62 percent of females. The kids themselves state that parents are "too worried about a small problem [pot]," and "more stress should be put on alcohol."

The Bureau of Substance Abuses in Boise, Idaho, surveyed almost half of the total school enrollment in junior and senior high schools in a certain region. The kids surveyed represented a group of 13- and 14-year-olds (51 percent) and 15- through 19-year-olds (49 percent). The results showed that at both age 13 and at age 18, alcohol was up to three times more popular than marijuana, the solidly second-place choice in almost every survey. A full 50 percent of the 18-year-olds drank regularly, while 20 percent of the 13-year-olds indicated usage of alcoholic beverages. Most parents will be surprised that 33 percent of the kids surveyed reported drinking alcohol *while in school*, not in drive-ins, parties, or other nonacademic environments. The summary of the survey states that "the results . . . establish the point that drugs are being used quite extensively by school-age children in Region VII."

The most popular drug: alcohol. Percentage using it between 13 and 18 years old: 50 percent.

In Mississippi, 33 percent of a sampling of 162 sixth-grade pupils—about 54 of them—reported they were regular "users" of alcoholic beverages, drinking somewhere between once a month and twice a week. More than half reported that their first drinking experience was in the home. They revealed that they drink mostly for taste, for fun, and to "go along with the crowd."

2

Legal Age—
Does It Matter?

On December 8, 1974, *The New York Times* reported that in New Jersey traffic-accident deaths rose to an all-time high in that year and that "one factor in the year-to-year rise appears to be a higher incidence of drinking and accidents among teenage drivers." The article said that since January 1, 1973, when the age of majority was cut from 21 to 18, 347,541 "potential drinking drivers" were added to the highways according to a State Police study. The report shows that 227 drivers in the 18-21 age bracket were involved in fatal accidents, up 25 from 1972, and that "16.6 percent of the group were either drunk or impaired." The previous year, the figure was 8.9 percent.

Does lowering the legal drinking age actually contribute to the increase in teen-age drinking itself? Most experts think it does, but a few warn against inaccurate statistics painting an invalid picture.

The highly touted National Highway Traffic Safety Administration survey released in early 1975 created quite a stir, slapping the collective wrist of those complacent state-house officials who have been telling us that there is "no evidence" of teen-age drinking problems in their state, or "no hard data" about the alleged increase in teen-age drinking. The study, capsulized and summarized and interpreted in newspapers throughout the country, was entitled "A Strategic Study for Communication Programs on Alcohol and Highway Safety—High School Study" and was prepared for the Office of Pedestrian and Driver Programs for the N.H.T.S.A. of the U.S. Department of Transportation. With that heavy title out of the way, let's take a look at the statistics.

According to the survey, *half of America's high school students go to drinking parties at least once a month, and a majority of them–61 percent–admit to getting drunk at least once a month.* That was the lead paragraph of a great many stories in the newspapers. Most of the stories went on to point out that the $100,000 study showed that:

—many teenagers say they have driven a car while they were "really pretty drunk."

—one-fourth said they have driven "once or twice" when they knew they were too drunk to drive.

—another one-fourth said they have driven *three or more* times when they knew they were too drunk to drive.

—a full 32 percent reported being a passenger in a car at least once a month with a "heavily drinking" driver.

—about 10 percent reported having consumed alcoholic beverages during the week they were interviewed, and *14 percent said they had drunk nine drinks or more!*

—15 percent said they had been drunk four or more times during the previous month.

—these drinking kids are not far-out dropouts or under-achieving alienated types, but come "from the mainstream of their classes."

These are some of the actual questions asked by the survey during the 95-minute interview with hundreds of kids from 25 areas selected to represent the entire nation.

In the past three months, were you in any social situation with young people and without adult supervision [in which] alcoholic beverages were consumed?

Fifty percent of the kids reported ARS (alcohol-related-situation) contact once a month or more.

How would you describe your family and your own social life?

A total of 67 percent of the ARS respondents said they were "quite close" or "very close" to their families, while 74 percent of the nondrinkers said the same—not much disparity. Fifty percent of the ARS kids "know a large circle of acquaintances," while 54 percent of the nondrinkers said the same.

If you had a personal problem that required confidential advice or assistance from another person, whom would you likely turn to?

Almost three-quarters of the kids—72 percent—said a "friend your own age," and 44 percent said "brother or sister." Only 36 percent said "parent," and only 9 percent said "teacher" or "clergyman." Only 11 percent said "relative," or "guidance counselor."

Psychological aspects of the survey are discussed in Part Two of this book. However, this seems to be the right time to mention some of the nonempirical conclusions that were made in the survey. One of the highlight statements is that in the current high school population, using alcohol in unsupervised peer social occasions is a "*large* and *pervasive* experience." Also, the survey states that "there is a group within this total population that is large (50 percent of all high school students) and frequently (once a month or more) involved in the alcohol-related situation which is a peer and unsupervised occasion.'' Further, the report says that 15 percent of the ARS-involved group are 15 years old or younger.

The survey states:

> "In general, the alcohol attitudes of the ARS-involved can be described as more "pro" drinking than the non-involved. They have very positive feelings about teen drinking and the social utility of alcohol. This is under-standable in the context of their parents' own use of alcohol which is considerably greater than the non-involved group.

The government survey shows that fully three-fourths of the ARS-involved students drank beer "most often," 9 percent drank wine, and only 12 percent drank liquor. As for the "reasons for drinking alcohol, where kids were asked to circle as many answers as applied, the survey revealed the following breakdown:

It helps me celebrate and have fun ------------------54%
I like the taste --52%
I like the feeling of getting high ---------------------36%
Because my friends drink ----------------------------27%
It makes me feel better about things ----------------23%
I feel more sure of myself --------------------------------9%
Because my parents don't want me to ----------------3%
I can dance better --------------------------------------3%

The majority (60 percent) of kids "have legal age friends to buy it" as the primary source of their alcohol; 26 percent smuggle it from their homes, and only 14 percent buy it themselves. Further, the favorite locations for drinking are *in a car* (their own or the family car) while driving around, or at the local hang-out—drive-ins seem popular. Peers are by far the most frequent drinking companions.

Are Teen-agers Drinking?

One of the interesting and shocking aspects of the survey is that the kids, for all of the "new awareness" and "with it" tags placed on their generation, are just as misinformed about drinking as their parents. A total of 81 percent agreed that "mixing different kinds of drinks can increase the effect of alcohol," and an equally depressing 75 percent believed that a can of beer is less intoxicating than an average mixed drink. (The figures for adults who believe these misconceptions are 80 percent and 65 percent, respectively.) Remember that one twelve-ounce can of beer contains the same *quantity* of alcohol as the average mixed drink: one ounce of 86-proof liquor.

Another shocker was that the kids who are drinking regularly in high school seem to be fully aware of the penalties and laws against underage drinking, possession, and so on, but remain undeterred by such. They agree that driving while intoxicated (DWI) is a key role in fatal car accidents, yet they do it (just like adults). They agree that it is generally the innocent victim who is killed in the DWI accident, yet they tend not to take action when involved with a drinking driver. They know what BAC means (blood alcohol concentration), know an owner of a store can be jailed or fined enormous amounts of money for selling alcohol to them, tend to know someone who has been stopped for possession (but few have heard of harsh consequences); yet they drink anyway. Even more than adults, they believe (wrongly) that cold showers and black coffee sober up a drunk person. Informed persons tell the joke about ending up with a wide-awake drunk, or a very wet one! (In Part Three we discuss some hard facts about alcohol and what it actually does in your body.)

About the N.H.T.S.A. report, Massachusetts Secretary of Public Safety Richard L. McLaughlin said he wasn't a bit surprised, and that it "simply confirmed everything that I've been telling people of the commonwealth for the past eighteen months. Teen-age drinking and driving has become a serious problem not only in Massachusetts but in most states across the nation, and we must begin to realize the true scope of the carnage."

McLaughlin went on to say that the number of fatal accidents triggered by teen-agers has risen 167 percent over the eighteen or so months between the time the law lowered the drinking age to 18 in March 1973, and the end of 1974. Arrests involving drinking teen-age drivers zoomed to 166 percent in the same period, he added. "I was dismayed at the findings of the study and at the fact that few people have realized how big a problem teen-age drinking is."

Dr. Matthew Dumont, Director of Drug Rehabilitation for the Massachusetts Department of Mental Health, said abuse of alcohol by "persons under 18 is growing at a frightening pace." He said that studies by him in 1973 showed more than *two-thirds* of Massachusetts children in grades 9 through 12 have been intoxicated one or more times the previous year. *And researchers indicate that studies for 1974 will show an even higher percentage!*

Dr. Dumont's views are corroborated by Rev. David A. Works, executive vice-president of the North Conway Institute, North Conway, New Hampshire. "There is no question that teen-age drinking has been on the increase over the past three or four years," Rev. Works said recently. "Every week now, I receive calls from anxious parents, from schools and churches, asking for advice on the problem." He said most of the callers who are teen-agers don't identify themselves as problem drinkers and still think of the "drinker" type as a skid row bum instead of someone who could be sitting next to them at school or asking them to dance at a party.

If the increase is alarming in such highly populated states as Massachusetts and Michigan, many experts feel it's equally obvious in some sparsely settled states, too. In Helena, Montana, Rep. Allen C. Kolstad introduced a bill calling for a referendum to amend the law allowing 18-year-olds to buy liquor legally. He reportedly supported raising the age to 19, because 18-year-olds, "particularly in high school," have generally abused the privilege. Citing many school administrators who had approached him on the subject, Kolstad said, "The main problem right now is that half of the high school students turn 18 years old before they graduate," and that this has tended to be a prime cause of the increasing death rate in teenage traffic accidents.

At the Sixth International Conference on Alcohol, Drugs, and Traffic Safety in Toronto, Canada in late 1974, two separate reports came to the same sobering conclusion regarding the increase in alcohol-related traffic accidents. Dr. Paul Whitehead, associate professor of sociology at the University of Western Ontario, and Dr. Wolfgang Schmidt, associate research director of the Addiction Research Foundation in Ontario, both concluded that since the drinking age was lowered from 21 to 18 years of age, "significantly more young drivers are being involved in accidents and are being killed, *and the carnage can be directly related to their drinking*—not to increased police sensitivity or across-the-board increases in traffic accidents."

"The problem of mixing drinking and driving is not new, but by making the purchase of alcoholic beverages legal for 18- to 20-year-olds, it possibly increased the proportion of them using alcoholic beverages, increased the frequency of drinking, and maybe even increased the amount of alcoholic beverage they consume at any one time," said Dr. Whitehead. He had studied police records for five years prior to June 1973, and reported that alcohol-involved collisions had their greatest increase among the 18-, 19- and 20-year-old age group. He added, almost parenthetically, that "dramatic" increases in alcohol-related accidents had also been charted for 16- and 17-year-olds.

In the year immediately following the age lowering, alcohol-related collisons among the 18 to 20-year-olds increased 174 percent, Dr. Whitehead's report said. This compares to the total collisions for that age group, which increased only 28 percent. In fact, he noted that the alcohol-related collisions was greater for 20-year-olds than for 24-year-olds (the control group) by *more than five to one!* And the total increase in collision cases in which the driver had been drinking was 300 percent among 18-year-olds, 348 percent among 19-year-olds.

Dr. Schmidt's report showed that the relaxation of legal controls on drinking was followed by "a rise in consumption and a rise in the damaging effects of drinking."

Indeed, in a national study undertaken by Toronto's Addiction Research Foundation, it was found with almost phenomenal consistency that since Canada lowered its legal drinking age to 18 in most provinces and territories and 19 in a few others, the incidence of alcohol-related traffic accidents and citations as well as problem drinking itself in that age group, has increased drastically. In metropolitan Toronto, for example, before the drinking age was reduced from 21 to 18, there were only 48 charges brought against 18- to 20-year-old drivers for impaired driving in 1970. In *only* the second half of 1971, the figure was 259, and for 1972 it had almost doubled to 457!

These are the "empirical observations" drawn by the Toronto group:

—a lower legal age results in a lower illegal age, because many teen-agers three or four years younger than the legal age could now "pass" for 18.

—more young people are drinking more.

—drinking/driving offenses among the young are increasing, while "other' alcohol offenses such as illegal possession are decreasing.

—the public has accepted the new laws and that, inasmuch as the lowered drinking age coincided with a lowered voting age, it would be "political suicide" for any politician to support any movement to return the drinking age to 21.

—people are "getting into trouble" with alcohol and seeking help for it at a younger age.

Joe Power, Coordinator of Community Organization with the Nova Scotia Commission on Drug Dependency, concluded, "There are certain trends we're seeing [these days], and one of them is that more and more younger people are getting into difficulty sooner. They're sophisticated about other drugs, but they're naïve about booze and the damage it might cause them . . . more and more are going to alcohol from other drugs."

But let's not look only at Canada—which is, after all, seemingly far ahead of the United States in making concerted studies of the drinking problems and habits among the young people of the country. Lowering the drinking age in some states in the United States has undoubtedly resulted in more traffic accidents. In a survey by *Alcohol and Health Notes*, a publication of the National Clearinghouse for Alcohol Information (of the National Institute of Alcohol Abuse and Alcoholism), Michigan and Rhode Island, after lowering the legal drinking age to 18, have reported a significant increase in teen-agers involved in traffic accidents while under the influence of booze. Five other states have lowered their legal drinking age to 18 or 20 since the federal government lowered the voting age in 1970, but those states claim no significant rise in alcohol-related traffic collisions.

How interesting then, to note that Maine's Department of Health and Welfare Commissioner Dean Fisher, M.D., doesn't think it has much of a teen-age drinking problem; yet at least one state senator has introduced legislation to return the legal drinking age from 18 to 20. In a response to a request for information concerning Maine's teen-age drinkers, planning associate Mel Tremper of the state's Bureau of Rehabilitation said, in part:

> I am sorry to say that I can offer little in the way of hard data. Except for a handful of reported admissions to general hospitals for medical complications associated with alcoholism, and a few admissions to small mental health centers, there is no official record of teen-age drinking problems in this state. Early returns from a survey of high school superintendents indicate that the superintendents either do not perceive any drinking problems among their students or are unwilling to admit their existence. . . . It is my belief, that, as yet, Maine is lagging behind the more urban areas of the country in the switch to increasing alcohol abuse among youth.

On the *exact date* as the one at the top of Tremper's letter, State Senator Walter Hitchens, was reported by the *Portland Express* to be introducing a bill raising the legal drinking age from 18 to 20 because of the alarming number of intoxicated teen-agers weaving down Maine's highways.

In West Virginia, the severity of the drinking problem among teen-agers was inadvertently mentioned in a statement by Bernard Clark of the West Virginia Highway Safety Administration. West Virginia lowered its drinking age from 21 to 18 in 1972. Clark now says there is no increase in teen-agers' alcohol-related traffic accidents in that state because "they no longer have to travel to neighboring states to buy their liquor." Connecticut officials are reported saying the same thing.

Teen-agers in that state used to drive to New York to buy their liquor before Connecticut lowered its own drinking age to 18 in October 1972.

The first and most common criticism of these surveys and statistical analyses is that statistics can prove anything. Very few statisticians will argue this point. In fact, most of us have heard the story about the statistician who drowned in a river whose average depth was only three feet!

In the interests of objectivity, it should be noted that many of the legal-drinking-age vs. drunk-driving traffic accidents and fatalities are somewhat skewed by certain facts and probabilities:

1. That such-and-such a statistic for teen-agers involved in alcohol-related traffic deaths in 1970, when the legal age for drinking was 21, may not account for (a) more drivers, and (b) more automobiles on the road, in a similar survey in 1974.

2. That a teen-age drunk-driving survey in 1974 cannot reflect in its tabular results the fact the policemen and other official recorders may not have recorded blood alcohol concentrations four years ago, nor might they have had the means to measure it accurately.

3. That terminology, semantics, and downright tricky phrasing can prove anything the surveyor wants to prove. In the words of Richard Zylman, a prominent and outspoken research specialist at the Center of Alcohol Studies at Rutgers University, "There is real danger that if we look for evil we will find it—even if it does not exist."

In a report presented at the National Alcoholism Forum of the Annual Conference of the National Council on Alcoholism in Denver in mid-1974, Mr. Zylman questions the validity of a Michigan report citing a 164 percent increase in "alcohol-involved fatal crashes" in the first quarter of 1973, immediately after the legal drinking age was lowered to 18, than in a similar period in 1971. Zylman suggests quite convincingly that the Michigan report actually showed a change in police reporting, rather than a change in drinking behavior. Zylman does note, however, in a report to the *Journal of Safety Research* of June 1973;

> In spite of the less significant role of alcohol in highway safety crashes involving youth, alcohol is related to youthful collision involvement in a way that sharply differentiates the young from the other age categories up to age 69. This concerns the impact of amall amounts of alcohol. *Among teenagers, low concentrations of alcohol are an important factor in crashes whereas in the 25-69 age groups such concentrations are of no statistical significance at all.*

In other words, Zylman states that teen-age drinkers can't handle their booze in driving situations as well as older groups, thus are more likely to have a crash. This is far more important to a parent—and as a nationally crucial problem—than whether a state survey of "alcohol-involved crashes" is accurate.

Finally, to give Zylman his due, in an article entitled "Over Emphasis on Alcohol May Be Costing Lives," published in *Police Chief* magazine in January 1974, he states that inaccurate figures in reporting "alcohol-related" traffic deaths may be making researchers too complacent about identifying *the major cause of fatal car crashes:*

> If we continue the obsession with alcohol as *the* major cause of crashes, trying to attribute ever-increasing numbers of traffic deaths to alcohol when the actual figure is around 30 percent, we may be blinding ourselves to the possibility that there are other major causes of traffic

crashes responsible for the other 70 percent of all traffic deaths, some of which may be even more important than alcohol.

He also states that the exaggerations of the alcohol aspect of traffic deaths in official surveys "reduce the credibility and, consequently, the supportability of programs to control alcohol-involved crashes."

Zylman's points are well taken. But the difference between 45 percent of all drivers responsible for multivehicle crashes ("popular and official belief," according to Zylman), and 42 percent (revealed by "research," also according to Zylman) is only 3 percent. We submit that 3 percent, *when identifying the problem of drinking among driving teen-agers* is not statistically significant.

The 60 percent of all single-vehicle crashes involving drunken drivers ("popular and official belief" again), and 57 percent ("research reveals") is also only 3 percent! We submit that this 3 percent, when identifying the problem of drinking among driving teen-agers is not statistically significant.

And we would also submit as a reminder—without dismissing Mr. Zylman's research and very cogent warnings —that at the Sixth International Conference on Alcohol, Drugs, and Traffic Safety in Toronto mentioned earlier, those two separate reports which concluded that "significantly more" young drivers had been involved in accidents and fatalities since the legal drinking age was lowered to 18 took pains to point out: "The carnage can be directly related to their drinking and not to increased police sensitivity or across-the-board increases in traffic accidents."

Granted, some studies look important upon first glance, but don't seem to produce much meaningful information regardless of how long they've been under way. For example, a study begun twenty-five years ago by Kaye Middleton Fillmore, an alcohol research specialist at Rutgers University, concluded that if you know the drinking habits of teen-agers and young adults, "you can make a pretty fair distinction about the problem drinking among them when they reach middle age," according to *Brewer's Digest* magazine. In an article reporting the results of the study, the magazine said Ms. Fillmore's study began "with data collected by two other researchers in 1949-52 on 17,000 students and in 27 colleges and universities. It continued in 1971-72 with her interviews 20 years afterward on about 200 of the same people."

Trouble is, Ms. Fillmore classified as "drinkers" anyone who had had one or more drinks over the past twelve months, which would discourage most casual and many serious investigators from giving credibility to the study, inasmuch as under normal circumstances every member of practically every family in America could be construed as a drinker. In any event, the report of the survey ends with the strong implication that Ms. Fillmore wants more money for follow-up studies. What a pity that 17,000 students at 27 colleges had been contacted and nothing more startling than the need for more follow-up studies resulted!

Nevertheless, the important thing in the continuing argument about whether the lowering of the drinking age contributes to traffic deaths is to realize that teen-age drivers are telling us that they are drinking more. Not traffic records, not the reports of insurance companies or accident-investigation policemen, but the *kids behind the wheels* are revealing that more and more they had been drinking at the time of the accident. No amount of including the children under 10 years of age in the overall traffic survey can change that fact. Not even if everyone ever involved in a crash were surveyed and the actual percentage of driver-drinking was shown to drop drastically to only 10 percent, could the significance of the fact that more teen-agers are driving while drunk be ignored any longer.

A good example is a survey taken by the Los Angeles

Are Teen-agers Drinking?

County Alcohol Safety Action Project (A.S.A.P.), conducted in 1973 as an extensive roadside survey, in which more than 1,000 drivers were asked to volunteer information about their drinking habits. The results are quite interesting, as a California teen-ager can drive at 16, but cannot drink until he's 21.

The Los Angeles A.S.A.P. survey showed that 76.9 percent of the driving 15-20 age group said they drink. The largest percentage of drinking respondents was between 21 and 39 years of age (84.6 percent and 82.8 percent, respectively). Drinking increased between 16 and 39, then tapered off.

The survey also showed the greatest percentage (25 percent) of the respondents consuming five or more drinks at a single sitting was the 15-20 age group. And that group, the teen-agers, showed by far the greatest percentage of in-home drinkers—85.2 percent—probably because of the illegality of getting booze anywhere else.

Teen-agers in general saw themselves as very light-to-fairly light drinkers (79.5 percent, the highest). Given the idea that 99 out of 100 problem drinkers do not think they are problem drinkers, and that 99 out of 100 heavy drinkers do not think they are heavy drinkers; this statistic is interesting. Emanda Miller of the Los Angeles A.S.A.P. reported:

> Our findings were pretty much as expected, because we'd run the study before and it doesn't appear the drinking/driving problem among young people is going down. We *were* surprised to see no ethnic differences, however. The sad thing is that we run these surveys and nobody listens to us. We seem to be the only group following through to try and do something about it, but it's like whistling in the wind. If there are no bucks in it, public officials won't wake up.

Kids Talk About
Their Drinking

Without attempting to psychoanalyze them or to explore their answers in depth to discern hidden meanings, we asked hundreds of teen-agers across the country to give us their feelings about their own drinking habits. Basic questions such as "Where did you get your booze?" and "How do your parents react to your drinking?" were asked, and in the peculiarly brief lexicon of the young, the kids told us what they thought. We present these responses—for the most part unedited—for those parents who find it difficult to accept the fact that there are millions of kids across the country who are addicted to alcohol. And we are presenting only a relatively few, because their comments become depressingly repetitious—an observation as significant as the responses themselves.

I wouldn't say I drink regularly, just whenever possible. My parents don't mind if I drink; they like it better than drugs, anyway. The reason I don't feel I need any help is because I really don't drink that much. I'm *only drunk* a few times a month. However, I have a friend who is only 15 and I can honestly say he's an alcoholic. He drinks in the morning, and he's drunk most of the time. I hassle him all the time but it doesn't do any good. He's even drunk at school a lot.

Jim, 15, California

I was with my father at home when I had my first drink. I guess I was 5 or 6 years old. You know, taking a sip of his beer whenever I could and him thinking I was cute or something. People noticed when I started drinking regularly because I would skip school to go get drunk and then when I went back to school I was drunk. I was 16 when I started drinking regularly. At first I would have someone older buy it for me, but then I started to go into beer joints and buy it myself with money I'd make from working. I didn't care about anything that happened to anybody; all I wanted to do was get drunk. I still drink now, but I've never asked anyone for help. I know my parents are scared, but they won't do anything. I think parents should be very harsh about drinking. I wish they could have stopped me so I wouldn't have a drinking problem now.

Brian, 17, Kansas

When we were 13, a bunch of us were riding around in a car and someone had some beer, so we all started drinking. All my friends drink. We just use our allowance and get an older guy to buy it for us. When my parents found out I was drinking, they really got mad. But I think if a kid knows when to quit drinking and doesn't get drunk, there's no reason for parents to get so upset.

Julie, 16, New York

One time, when I was about 13, me and my friend were up in this guy's bedroom and we were trying to get a couple of girls drunk. I had two bottles of Boone's Farm and a little vodka myself, so it didn't do me any good when the girls did get drunk. My friends and I can get all the booze we want—we just rip it off at the party store. My parents don't know anything about my drinking, but if they ever find out, I think they should act sensibly about it.

Matt, 16, New Jersey

The most I ever drank was every weekend during the summer when I was about 13. I like to drink—it makes me feel giggly. I don't think my parents know I drink away from home, but I think they realize that every kid drinks while growing up and they just have to accept it.

Therese, 16, California

By the time I was 15, I was drinking regularly. I guess my parents knew about it because sometimes when I came home I acted kind of funny. I never got totally wiped out—just kind of funny. Drinking makes me feel happy and helps me have a good time. I have to be honest and admit that sometimes it makes me sick, though. My parents told me they don't like me to drink at parties, but they're cool. My mother will even buy for me if a real special event comes up. Parents just have to teach their kids to drink sensibly and set a good example.

Maureen, 17, California

I went to my first party when I was 14 with a bunch of friends who had been to lots of parties before. I didn't want to look square, so I started drinking. That's the only time I drink, at parties. We have them about once a month and we all chip in to buy the beer. I guess I get kind of fuzzy when I drink, and I'll laugh at everything. My mother caught me drinking once and she was really pretty upset and hurt. She said that if I wanted to ruin my life, then it was up to me. I guess I would be pretty hurt too if I caught *my* daughter drinking behind my back.

Michelle, 16, Illinois

When I was 13, a bunch of us organized a big party and that's when I had my first drink. I guess I'd say I was drinking pretty regularly by the time I was 15. My parents don't have a clue though; they always figure I'm at a school dance or a game and the subject just never come up. I know how I think parents should react to their kids drinking—harsh and with enforcement.

Janice, 16, Michigan

In the ninth grade we celebrated Christmas vacation with a party and I had my first drink. By 15, I was drinking all the time. My parents don't know about my drinking though, because I always sober up before going home.

"Madame X," 17, Connecticut

I had my first real drink on a camp-out when I was 15. Now I only drink on weekends and at parties where we usually all chip in and get the oldest kid to buy. I always feel pretty happy when I'm drinking, but the next day I feel like shit.

Bob, 18, Michigan

A bunch of us chipped in on some liquor for a party and had my friend's brother buy it for us. I was about 11 then. After a few drinks, I really felt pretty confident. I only drink once in a while, and my parents get pretty mad when I do. I think they should talk to me more about what could really happen from drinking. But they just get mad; they don't talk to me.

Kevin, 14, Illinois

Three years ago I was really a heavy drinker. I used to get smashed almost every night until my parents got scared and sent me away to live with a relative in a small town. I didn't have a drink for a whole year and I had a great time. Nowadays I only drink about once every two weeks.

Stan, 17, Canada

I can't stand being stoned, so I don't drink that much. Just enough at a party to make me feel tipsy so I relax. Everyone drinks Southern Comfort—it's the favorite. When we have company at home, my dad will offer me a sherry before dinner, and if he's not looking, my mother will mix me a gin and tonic because she knows I like that better.

Karen, 16, Virginia

My parents noticed I was drinking when I was about 16, and they didn't like it at all. In fact, they tried to keep me home so I wouldn't go to parties. I guess that's the way parents should react, though. I always use my own money to buy booze, and my friends or my cousins get it for me. Most of the time when I drink, I feel more sociable and happy, but sometimes it makes me feel real sad.

Lori, 17, Oregon

I don't consider myself a "drinker"—I just drink wine every week. When I was 16, my parents let me drink at home. That's the way it should be. It shouldn't be that big a deal. If parents make liquor available to their kids, they won't want to sneak out and try it.

Gerald, 19, California

I really get mad when I hear parents, who have wine every night with dinner or beer with TV, talk about kids and drugs. A lot of adults think drugs is anything that kids use. They don't use "drugs." They forget about all their prescriptions and their nightly martini. Boy, you should see some of the heavy stuff in our medicine cabinet.

Joan, 14, New York

When I was about 7, my dad started letting me have beer whenever I wanted it. I guess I was a pretty regular drinker by the time I was 13. That's when my parents noticed—all our neighbors were talking about it. My parents don't want me drinking behind their backs, but they're the ones who started me in the first place, so they shouldn't complain. Drinking really relaxes me. Whenever we want to have a party, we just take up a collection and stand outside a liquor store watching for a buyer.

Chris, 15, Michigan

One night my buddies and I were drinking beer in a parked car and the cops caught us. No big deal—I just got caught that's all. I guess I've been drinking ever since I got into high school. Man, everyone at my school drinks—if not a lot, then a little something on a regular basis.

Steve, 17, Washington

Every weekend, and sometimes oftener, my crowd goes drinking. We pool our money and get the stuff through our "source," or else we bring bottles from home. Then we go to wherever the parents are gone. Nothing much happens. We just drink, make out, once in a while somebody passes out. The youngest kid in our crowd is 13, but she's very advanced for her age. So are the rest of us. Most teen-agers drink—you don't have much fun without it.

Ed, 15, New Jersey

My regular drinking started in the eighth grade. My parents

never knew because I never came home loaded. My older sister usually bought the stuff for me. I paid for it with my allowance. I like to drink; it makes me feel buzzy.

Dan, 18, Texas

My aunt gave me my first can of beer when I was about 14, and that started it. My friends pressured me a little, but not much. I just drank 'cause I felt like it. I only spend about $2.50 a week for booze which I buy myself. All my friends buy their own and we pool it all. A lot of them have summer cabins and sometimes when the parents won't be there, we'll all go out to the country for a big party. Not many people who don't drink go to these parties 'cause they feel so left out. Of the twenty or thirty kids who go, about a third of them are heavy drinkers. That's pretty much why I go—to drink. We can handle our booze, though. We have about five drinks each—that's all. About a third of a glass of bourbon and the rest Coke or some other mixer. I like mine strong. But I don't like vodka—it makes me sick. I don't see anything wrong with drinking, as long as you don't need more and more each time you drink.

Gail, 17, Georgia

My friends didn't really *pressure* me to have a drink, they just sort of coaxed me. But I didn't *have* to take it if I didn't really want to. This happened at a seventh-grade party. By the time I was 13, I was a pretty regular drinker. My elder brother used to buy it for me, but then he got worried because I was drinking more and more whiskey. When I first started drinking, I felt more sociable, more "in." But then no one was noticing I was drinking, so I started drinking more and more just to get attention. I never got any professional help or anything. I just had a long talk with a real close friend, and after that I decided to cut down. A few things happened that really scared me in my freshman and sophomore years of high school. One time I

57

found myself twenty miles from home and I didn't know how I got there. And several times I found myself in a strange house. I just got sick and tired of puking from too much whiskey and not knowing what I did the night before. So without even going to A.A. or some other counseling or anything, I resolved to cut out the hard stuff and only drink beer socially. That's all I drink now, and then only on weekends and at parties. My parents were really insecure. They were ashamed of me and worried about what the neighbors and relatives would think if they found out about my drinking. I wish they hadn't been so blinded by their own thoughts of being disgraced by having an alcoholic kid. If they knew how common the problem was, they wouldn't have been so shocked.

Karen, 16, California

When we were 10, my friends and I went to the woods behind the playground and drank some beer. When I was 13, I was drinking every weekend. We used to pay winos to buy our booze. They were always ready to make a few extra cents. I don't think I have a drinking problem. My folks think I'm a drunk, though.

Mark, 20, Virginia

The only reason I drink is to get high. I don't even like the taste of the stuff. And I certainly wouldn't waste my money on booze if I was just thirsty—I'd drink water. If you're going to drink, you've got to do it up big. I drink to get high, and that's the only reason.

Tami, 16, California

My dad is always bitching about my drinking, but strange as it seems, he was the one who got me started—I was 14. My brother drank and so did all my friends, so who was to say anything about it? It's easy to get booze. Just stand in front of a liquor store until someone older comes along and ask them to buy for you. I use my paper-route money. My parents aren't really strict about my drinking—they just bitch a lot. They never *discussed* it with me. By the time they were through yelling, I needed a drink.

Matt, 17, New York

My parents are cool about my drinking, especially during the summer. We have this summer cabin, and whenever they're there my folks are really loose. I can stay out all night and they never say anything. I guess it's just the atmosphere —everything is so relaxed and all. Most of my friends drink, and most of the parents don't seem to mind. If you smoked dope, they'd mind. Then it would be another story. They would automatically think you were selling it, or something worse.

Cindy, 16, California

I guess I'm awfully messed up. My father died when I was 8 and my mother is a crazy lady. I left school at 16 and trained as a nurse's aide, but I flunked out. I also failed as a bank clerk and a waitress. I was too nervous, and I couldn't take the discipline. I started drinking just to calm myself. My husband just left me because he couldn't stand to live with a drunk. The hell with him—why should I give up booze? What else have I got going for me?

Jan, 18, California

My father has a drinking problem, so I know what alcohol can do to a person. If parents want to help their children, they shouldn't drink either, because if they drink and tell their kids not to drink, they're just contradicting themselves.

Nancy, 15, Michigan

Are Teen-agers Drinking?

I'm just a social drinker. My friends and I often have a couple of drinks in a downtown bar—they serve us all the time. I once asked my father what he would say if the bar were raided. He said, "So the place gets busted. Be smarter next time."

Brenda, 16, Canada

I like getting drunk better than getting stoned. When I get stoned, it really burns me out the next day, and it's hard for me to concentrate, especially at school. I stay away from dope, except for maybe on the weekend. I very rarely get a hangover with booze. I guess sex plays a role in drinking, but when I'm drinking I just sort of feel whatever happens happens. My parents are so unaware. When I was using drugs, my whole personality changed. I was withdrawn and messed up. I was buzzing all the time, and my parents didn't even notice. They'd rather have me drink than take dope. When I go to a party my mom would sometimes say, "You know I don't care what you drink. Just make sure if there's any dope there, you don't smoke it." Drinking's cool, though. When I got up the other morning after a party, my dad asked me what time I got home. I told him 2:30 or 3:00, and he said, "That's kind of early, isn't it?" Then he asked me if I had a hangover and I said no. He asked me if I got drunk and I said, "Wellll. . . " He said, "That's cool—don't worry." My mom just sort of looked at me and asked, "How's your head?" I thought to myself, "Hey, wait a minute—that's not the way parents should act when their daughter tells them something like this!" My parents really trust me, though. I'm kind of on a tightrope. I want to do my own thing, but I don't want to do anything that will hurt them.

Debbie, 19, California

I guess I had trouble with drinking when I was about 14. I would start my day with four or five shots of whiskey before going to school in the morning. It was a great escape. I was terror-stricken in school. I felt like people didn't like me or that I had nothing to offer. Escaping through drugs allowed me to be somebody I wasn't. My parents didn't care. They said, "As long as it's legal, that's all we worry about." They don't even realize that alcohol overdoses outnumber heroin overdoses ten to one. I read that in the newspaper.

Fred, 16, Colorado

My drinking resulted in trouble from the very first. I threw a rock through a liquor store window once to get some stuff, and I had my first real binge when I was only a sophomore. I also had my first blackout. I drank all through high school, whenever the opportunity presented itself. I managed to secure a phony I.D. when I was 15 so I could get the stuff whenever I wanted. When I turned 16 and got a car, I was mixing drinking with driving. I don't have to tell what happened. Now that I'm in college I'm a swinger—you're either an athlete or a swinger—and I'm certainly no athlete.

Al, 21, California

At 13 I was sent to live with an uncle in Nevada because my stepfather and I just couldn't get along. He felt that if, at an early age, you became aware of your capacity for booze, you wouldn't have any trouble with it later. So I had the freedom to drink anything in the house. I enjoyed drinking from the start and didn't seem to have any problems. But I kept getting into trouble. By the time I was 17, I was in reform school, twice. Drinking played a larger and larger part in my life. When I experienced my first blackouts, I was kind of worried, but then I just accepted them as a normal part of life. By the time I was 21 everything revolved around my drinking.

Jim, 22, New York

61

Are Teen-agers Drinking?

I was drinking sloe gin and taking pills regularly when I was 9. I could always get booze—I'd just stand in front of a liquor store and ask a nice older gentleman or a young guy to buy me a six-pack for our party. I never had to wait long, either. I liked scotch and ice-cold beer in a bottle. I drank to get drunk, every weekend at least. I knew I had a problem, but I didn't want to identify myself as an alcoholic because I didn't want to be what my mother was. A lot of kids drink because they're afraid of pills or acid, and they never think it will hurt them. They think, "How can I be an alcoholic when I'm only a kid—you have to be at least 40."

Jane, 18, California

At 13, I drank to get drunk. I was afraid of getting busted with pot, so I just switched to something legal. There was a group of four of us, and I think we were all alcoholics. We used to carry small scotch bottles, you know, the kind you get on airplanes. We would dump it in our Cokes or soda and we could get mildly loaded anytime we wanted. On a typical day I would get up, stop at a friend's and sniff some glue, hair spray, or anything in an aerosol can. Then I'd go to school. During break we'd load our milk with our scotch and drink that. Then after school we'd all go to a friend's house and have a few drinks. Then home again and if my parents went out, I would go back to sniffing glue or try an aerosol high. Then I'd pass out, sleep, and start all over again the next day. It's surprising how you can do that all the time without your parents catching on.

Ben, 19, California

From the very first drink I was hooked. That was when I was 15. I never drank socially. I drank to get drunk, as often and as much as I could. My eventual goal was to drink myself to death. I had been so unhappy, lonely, and scared for so long that the discovery of booze seemed the answer to all my problems. I was always drunk. My parents' car had a strong attraction to fences, and one night I blacked out and drove the car down a bank, ramming a steel fence around someone's back yard. This scared me so much it gave me another excuse to have another drink. I lost my driver's license and was put on probation. When it became obvious school was interfering with my drinking, I did the only logical thing—ran away from home. I was hitching around the country for a month. Then I drank to ease my conscience and forget what I had done. There's always some excuse.

Lisa, 18, Washington

Even when I was a little kid, I used to sneak sips of booze from my parents' drinks when they weren't looking. I used to think drinking was a big thing—real he-men drank. All my cowboy heroes drank. I used to put scotch in my milk Thermos in junior high school and I even stole altar wine when serving mass. By age 13, I needed alcohol just to get out of bed in the morning. I had the shakes and cold sweats every day. I had my next-door neighbor buy the stuff for me. He was a college kid and he had a heavy drug habit to support, so I paid him to buy it for me. I spent about three months in my room drunk, and one day I put a .45-caliber revolver into my mouth and pulled the trigger. But I was so drunk I had forgotten to load the gun. At this point I realized how bad things were and called one of the self-help phone numbers my mother had been leaving around the house.

Jess, 18, California

I became a casual drinker when I was 13. I was old for my age and hung around with older kids. They'd give me the odd bottle of beer or a swig from the wine bottle, and it seemed like a smart thing to do. My consumption gradually increased, and before I knew it, if I didn't have something to drink every day I missed it. I guess I discovered one day that I felt better when I was drinking. Drinking didn't make me happy, but it took the edge off of my shyness and loneliness. I don't know why, but when I was sober I always felt lonely and shy. By the time I was 15, I was drinking heavily—maybe a bottle or two of wine a day or a case of beer or a mickey of rye whiskey. I would drink in alleys, in parks, behind buildings. Sometimes I would arrive in the classroom in the morning smashed. I celebrated my 16th birthday by being drunk most of the following week. By then I craved alcohol. Being drunk helped me forget that I was me. Blessed oblivion, as they say. I transferred from high school to a trade school, and before long I dropped out completely. I took odd jobs to earn money to buy booze. I also got booze money by buying stuff for young kids from the liquor store or brewer's retail. I was well-built for a 16-year-old and could pass for 18 or 19. My parents knew and tried to help me, but I couldn't accept their love. I stumbled through my seventeenth year like a zombie. One time I woke up to find my clothes in shreds and my skin lacerated in several places. I'd had a fight with a large German shepherd dog. When I turned 18, I swore I would give up drinking. But after a day or two the withdrawal symptoms—nervousness, nausea, weakness, trembling, sweating, and stomach pain—were so bad that I could no longer endure and went back to the bottle. I'm ashamed, really ashamed, of the things I did during those four years. What I regret most was all the worry and hurt I gave to my parents and my two younger brothers. I did terrible things. I beat up people, for no good reason, who were my friends. I told lies. I hid from the police. I dropped out of school. I ruined my body by drinking huge amounts of wine, beer, vodka, or whiskey—anything with alcohol in it. I finally realized that I had reached rock bottom and went for help.

Gino, 19, Ohio

PART TWO

WHY DO OUR TEEN-AGERS DRINK?

*Fill all the glasses there, for why
Should every creature drink but I,
Why, man of morals, tell me why?*
    —Abraham Cowley, DRINKING, 1656

The Major Influences on
Teen-Agers' Drinking

Any good book about teen-age drinking is supposed, by some unwritten rule, to have a section devoted to exploring the question of why teen-agers drink. Any interested parent can find whole books on this subject, written by psychologists, psychiatrists, counselors, educators, clergymen, and other "experts" all of whom have their own pet theories and intellectual rationale. But in all the literature on the subject, the closest anyone has ever come to the *truth* of why kids drink is the statement that kids drink for the same reasons adults drink.

Consequently, most of the literature devoted to kids and alcohol is practically useless to the layman either because it often takes a specific theoretical viewpoint and then beats it into the ground, or else is so bound up in unintelligible jargon and clinically confounding esoterics that most of the usable information is lost to the everyday reader. So unless you can sit down with a knowledgeable person, or spend a few hours with a communicative professional, exploring the pre-1975 literature can be a waste of time for the parent seeking to learn why kids drink.

One would think that asking the kids themselves would afford some insight. In fact, it does afford *some*, but it isn't deep or thoughtful enough to be of any practical use. (A parent cannot, for example, do much with "Because it's a kick in the head.") It should be remembered that a teen-ager, almost by definition, is not mature enough and does not have the psychological insight for an accurate evaluation of the reasons behind his drinking habits.

Art Cole, a Public Information Director for Alcoholics Anonymous in Los Angeles, says:

> Kids don't really have the life experience behind them to make a choice—a moral choice—a decision about what is the best thing to do. Kids who are problem drinkers are used to acting older than they really are, and when dealing with these kids you have to remember that they really are just that—kids. Chronologically they're just teen-agers, not the mature adults they try to act like. So, you can't expect a teen problem drinker to act like an adult problem drinker. He doesn't have the background to make the decision that he needs help, so you couldn't possibly ask him to make the very profound analysis of why he drinks in the first place."

Any exploration of the statement, "Kids drink for the same reasons adults drink," should not be made without first acknowledging the next logical question: "Okay, then why do *adults* drink?" This leads to the question of *why* we have to know *why*. Isn't it true that kids drive a car for the same reason adults drive a car? That kids have picnics for the same reason adults have picnics? That kids kiss for the same reason adults kiss? That kids fight for the same reason adults fight? Why aren't there books written about *why* adults drive? About *why* adults have picnics? This *reductio ad absurdum* finally ends with the question of what's wrong with drinking in the first place.

Nothing, when it is done in "moderation." Keeping in mind that what's "moderate" for one person may be poisonous overindulgence for another, there are some arguments put forward in favor of drinking. In *Young People and Drinking* (John Day Company, 1968), Dr. Arthur H. Cain lists seven:

1. The moderate use of wine was acceptable in biblical days, and it was regarded as a gift from God, to be used wisely and well. (The phrase "Only God makes wine; all we do is coddle it" will someday dawn upon some advertising copywriter and his firm will make a fortune for some vineyard or other.)

2. Drinking is an old social custom which has permitted people to relax together and become more friendly.

3. Alcoholic beverages have been, and still are, widely used at the table for the family's mealtime drink.

4. Wine has been, and still is, in some countries, a substitute for water and milk.

5. Moderate drinking is a relatively harmless way of relaxing in a tense world.

6. Moderate, "civilized" drinking may be an index of mature behavior and serve as a symbol of adulthood among many social groups.

7. The normal use of alcohol may indicate a person's all-around good health and normalcy.

All right. If "kids drink for the same reason adults drink," we might assume that a kid can drink to relax, to be socially amenable, to keep from drinking our polluted water, to show his adult maturity, to aid digestion, and even to prove that he can handle it so his parents will get off his back. Adults will give you all the same reasons a kid will for their drinking. In "Exploring Alcohol Questions" (a leaflet from Rutgers University's Center of Alcohol Studies), Raymond G. McCarthy says:

> People who drink beer, wine or distilled spirits give various explanations for their action. Some drink for the taste and flavor; others for the relaxing effect of alcohol; still others to experience the extreme change in the way they feel about themselves and their surroundings. There are individuals who seek intoxication.

We may also assume that if "kids drink for the same reasons adults drink," the so-called "value crisis" is getting to them just as it's getting to many adults. Our world is in the midst of a severe change of morals and ethics. Changes over the last twenty-five years have greatly increased the complexities and anxieties of life, and the options available to each of us have multiplied. Anyone born since World War II has been steadily bombarded with the threat of atomic weapons: air raid drills in school, fallout shelters in neighborhoods, large corporations offering cut rates to employees who bought and stocked bomb shelters—remember? Remember the instructions that told you which Conelrad radio stations to turn to "in the event of an emergency"? Ask your children—they remember, too.

Is it any wonder that our own insecurities and fears are being matched by those of our children? Add that our kids have more money, more time and more freedom than we did, and you've got a nice corollary. "Kids drink for the same reason adults drink," and "kids find it *easier* to drink than adults did at the same age." Social life today begins at 12 or

13 years of age, not 16 or 17 as in our generation or 21 or 22 as in our parents' day, yet the morals and values of the adult world are still expected to be embraced by this new "social" group of youngsters. They still—and probably always will —ape their parents. But they're only 12 and 13, *not* 16 and 17. Our important status symbols and material possessions which we revere become theirs, too.

Farfetched? Hysterical? Not really. The evidence indicates that teen-age drinking is a *reflection of the drinking habits of adults and of the attitude of adults towards drinking.* The fact that most adults regard alcohol as a recreational beverage rather than a drug is reflected in the attitudes of the teen-agers. Only when adults start regarding alcohol as a toxic drug can a sound, effective alcohol education program for America's youth begin.

When marijuana smoking came out from behind closed doors in the sixties, tremendous pressures were brought to bear on America's teen-agers. Tough drug laws were dusted off and applied no longer only to "dope fiends" and hard drug pushers, but also to the casual experimenter. Because American parents could not consider that alcohol might be more toxic and poisonous than marijuana, a kid caught with a six-pack of beer in his car was sent home with a reprimand, but one caught smoking a joint could be accused of a crime only slightly less serious than armed robbery. Parents who hardly ever drew a sober breath on weekends panicked at the idea of their kids being "on drugs," and most assumed that a drag on a joint was the first step down the road to narcotics addiction that could only be supported by prostitution, pimping, and burglary. But a 13-year-old coming home drunk on booze from a party was regarded as just a "normal incident" in the oh-so-trying process of puberty and growing up.

The chief problem, obviously, is that alcohol *is* a drug,

just like heroin or cocaine, and legal. (Actually, it might be helpful to think of alcohol as an anesthetic, like ether. It works much the same way.)

Consider this imaginary conversation between you and your son or daughter:

"Dad? Have you ever mainlined on heroin?"

"No, sir! That stuff's habit-forming. You could become a dope addict forever!"

"Dad? Have you ever sniffed coke?"

"No, sir! Bad stuff! You could become a dope fiend! It's illegal!"

"Have you ever blown grass?"

"No, sir! That stuff's bad. Oh, I know they say it isn't habit-forming, but it's *illegal*!"

"Have you ever gotten smashed on gin?"

"Why, er, yes, I suppose so. But that's *legal*."

"Okay, Dad. Just wanted to check. Pass the gin!"

Maybe a bit ludicrous when put so openly, but really not far from the truth, because time and time again, when asked why they took their first drink or why they considered continuous drinking not to be too potentially dangerous, teen-agers are almost unanimous in their response: *If it's okay for my folks, it can't be too bad for me.*

An easy way to determine the validity of various theories on why kids drink to excess is to collect articles, interviews, and case histories. From all over the nation, from every expert we could find, and from hundreds of kids in many states, we set down everything we could get, then categorized it.

Four stacks of information formed, and the pile marked PARENTAL INFLUENCE was at least four times higher than the second-place pile. FOR EFFECT. Here, then, in order, are the most popular reasons why teenagers drink:

The Major Influence on Teen-agers' Drinking

1. Teen-agers drink because of some parental influence: either to appear "grown up," or because they see parents drinking in "legal" or "acceptable" conditions or because the repercussions are less serious with booze than with, say, pills or marijuana, or because some elements of this society actually encourage them to drink.

2. Teen-agers drink "for the effect": to get high, to rebel, to alter their feelings or their environment, if only temporarily.

3. Teen-agers drink because of peer pressure: for all their talk of "freedom," "preservation of individuality," and "being treated like a person," teen-agers are the most severe conformists of all; they are insecure.

4. Teen-agers drink because of emotional disturbances.

Kids Drink Because of Parental and Social Influences

I guess I really started when I was about 11. Oh, I tasted beer from Dad's mug when he watched ball games on TV—all kids do that. And when they had parties, people used to let me taste their drinks—I never liked the straight stuff, but I remember the white drinks were fun. I now know what I called the "white" drinks as a small kid were the gin- and vodka-tonics. Anyway, when I was about 11, I used to start stealing it. You know, taste a little when they weren't home, or maybe I was looking forward to tasting some of my friends' Thermos jugs at lunchtime in school. Then one time my father really got mad and really beat me up—I was 14—when I really blew it and came home drunk one night. But I don't think he would have hit me so much if he'd been sober himself.

Marcy, 16

74

Many psychologists will tell you that when people are afraid to use the word "alcoholic" in connection with teen-agers, it's because they're anxious about their own drinking habits. Notice how some of your more problematical drinking friends react to your substitution of the word "alcohol" for the word "drink." Ask them, "Would you like some alcohol?" instead of "Would you like a drink?" and note the negative reaction. Instead of "Have you got anything to drink?" ask "Got any alcohol?" The idea is that most adults—and especially parents—absolutely refuse to consider alcoholism as anything other than the skid row bum's affliction. When applied to themselves, they'll substitute every euphemism they can find to avoid the terms "alcoholic" or "alcoholism," and when discussing the drinking behavior of teen-agers or pre-teens, "alcoholism" seems utterly incredible. Most of the time, it's the drinking parents who'll cringe fastest at the word, maintaining that alcoholism is a grown-up's disease, but one that could never afflict *them*. Alcoholism is no different in nature from an allergy, a neurosis, a chronic skin problem, claustrophobia or habitual smoking—except, of course, that its capability of killing you is a lot higher.

The problem seems to be not so much that parents *condone* drinking because they do it themselves and because it's *legal*, but that parents actually seem to glorify drinking in many cases. We brag about how much we can drink, and in the process make drinking attractive: the man who does forty pushups before he goes to bed—even though crocked—is admired by his wife; the man who brags about how well he can drive, even though smashed, is smiled upon; the man who can drink seven drinks and "not even feel it" is admired for his stamina and virility. Our cowboy heroes took a shot at the bar to "steady their nerves" for the big shoot-out at high noon, and even such a nice man as Shane was laughed at and ridiculed by the tough guys when he ordered sarsaparilla for his little friend. Hard-drinking he-men pervade our folklore, and "two-fisted drinkers" are glamorized in song and legend. And all this is drummed into our youth at a time when their own values are in a constant state of flux, when they are not so sure what, after all, is *really* right and wrong in a rapidly changing world. Is the teetotaler a pansy, or strong-willed and sensible? Is it true you cannot trust a man who doesn't drink? Is the drunken surgeon who mutters "get me some coffee—*black* coffee!" and then performs a prefrontal lobotomy for the morning TV watchers to be emulated and admired? Is the moderate drinker a "square" who isn't much fun and should be dropped off the invitation list to the next raucous party?

It's up to parents to decide, and then to pass those decisions on via the models they provide for their children.

National statistics state that 7 out of 10 young people under the age of 14 have tasted alcohol, and most often it has been in the home, with parental permission. One official of A.A. said that parents often unconsciously encourage their children to drink by seeming to be almost proud of it when the child drinks. "Some parents even think it's cute for a youngster to get drunk at a party with adults," he added.

Dr. Morris Chafetz says, "Parents understand alcohol. It's 'their' drug. But I am greatly disturbed at the number of parents who are relieved when their children switch from pot to alcohol. Alcoholism, drunkenness, is a drug overdose." He also mentions that some drinking children are imitating their parents when they drink, trying to be "grown up." Because of this the kids often see nothing wrong with excessive drinking. He says:

> Alcohol has completely permeated our national life. We can't socialize without it, and the kids realize this subconsciously. They know that when someone offers

their Dad a drink, that someone doesn't mean water or Coca-Cola. And the kid knows his parents go to cocktail parties, to which his mother wears a cocktail dress. He's told when he becomes a man, he can drink with them to celebrate his manhood. We are constantly highlighting for the child the importance of alcohol in this society.

Further, Dr. Chafetz, who drinks moderately, acknowledges the "thank God he's not on drugs" syndrome.

Parents who learn their children are not using the so-called "hard" drugs are relieved they're "only" using alcohol. And while we are not getting into a competitive battle with other drugs, but a comparative one, parents are being relieved into a serious situation. Since no drug comes close in any measurement to the human and social destruction of alcohol problems, these parents are being relaxed into a situation that is like jumping from the frying pan into a bonfire.

This "relief" can be dangerous in and of itself. Listen to the testimony of Norma, a member of Al-anon, the organization for families of alcoholics. Norma has a daughter who is a stunning blonde, who became a fashion model at 16 after dropping out of school because of alcoholism, and then lost that job and several others because of her drinking.

She started on grass before she was 15 years old, and when she switched to alcohol I was relieved. I didn't consider alcohol to be as bad as marijuana. I drank, so I thought I could teach her to drink properly. I told her, "Don't drink alone, don't drink two strong drinks in a row, don't drink in the morning." Finally, I realized that the don'ts didn't help. It was a hassle for my girl to get pills and pot, but people rush to give her drinks. Everyone expects you to drink. It's sad. Drinking's serious, yet it's the topic of so much humor. Alcohol abuse is accepted in our society.

Sometimes it's so "accepted," parents actually feel an obligation to supply their kids with alcohol. In *Tonight Is Too Late*, Thelma Purcell tells of a California mother who supplied a keg of beer for her son's party; when trouble occurred, she got angry with the judge for "singling her out." She felt all parents were "doing the same thing," and why should she be the only one who got punished by the law? Ms. Purcell also recounts the case of the 17-year-old Connecticut student who was killed in an automobile accident after spending an evening visiting teen-age parties in the homes of two prominent families. Both parties served liquor, and the driver of the car was charged with negligent homicide. When the case came up before a judge, he ordered the arrest of all the hosts of the parties and their hired bartenders, quoting a state law that says "any person, except parent or guardian of a minor, who delivers or gives liquor to a minor, except on order of a physician, shall be subject to penalties." The hosts were outraged and the town got up in arms. The population thought the judge was being "unnecessarily just" and he became the target of anonymous phone calls and public insults. He was finally forced to install an unlisted telephone.

A junior high school teacher in Newport News, Virginia, believes so-called "cool" parents are the biggest source of alcohol for kids. "They give it to the kids as a bribe," he says. "The deal is 'promise that you won't do any dope and I'll buy you another bottle of vodka.' "

Norm Southerby, of the Los Angeles County Alcoholic Safety Action Project (A.S.A.P.), has reported that one couple in California experienced such anguish because their

19-year-old daughter had been using pot and pills that when their younger daughter started drinking they were actually relieved. "She'd get so drunk she would be throwing up in the morning, yet her parents were unconcerned," he said.

A superintendent of public schools in Pennsylvania agrees, citing the same tiresome phrase: "I get parents in here to talk about an incident involving their kid drinking, and the first thing they say is, 'Thank God, it's not drugs!' "

"We find a lot of parents who actually congratulate their kids for floundering with alcohol instead of other drugs that are considered dirty or illegal," says Larry Metzger, a California psychiatric counselor at an alcoholism clinic. "A lot of kids who are tired of worrying about drug busts and bad trips are turning to liquor—to the relief of their parents—and they are right in step with the hip fashion of drinking nowadays. And it's hard for these young people to realize their problem is real when they've dropped an illegal hang-up and picked up a socially approved one."

According to Dr. Mary Kubiak, head of the alcoholism treatment unit at the Winnebago Mental Health Institute near Milwaukee: "Kids learn from their parents. We're a drinking society." Dr. Kubiak was reported in the *Milwaukee Journal* as believing that "the same parents who tolerate drinking in the home would be appalled to find their children using LSD or marijuana. What they don't realize is that alcohol is one of the most dangerous drugs because its withdrawal symptoms can be more severe than those of narcotics, if not handled properly." The same story indicated that school officials in the Milwaukee area, who are sending drunken children home from school in greater numbers than ever before, are asking professionals to increase local programs on alcoholism for parents, apparently because it is generally recognized that parental attitudes are the primary influence on teen-age drinking habits. According to Dr. Seldon Bacon, Director of the Center of

Alcohol Studies at Rutgers University, "Drinking is a custom—it is a learned 'way' of a named group of people."

Recently a state official of New Jersey, reporting that the war against drug abuse in his state was, at best, a stalemate, called parental influence and attitudes toward drinking "one of the most difficult causes to overcome."

Matthew P. Boylan, director of the New Jersey division of Criminal Justice, was quoted in the *Newark Star-Ledger* earlier this year:

> Once a kid leaves illicit drugs, he sometimes finds that he needs something else to fill the vacuum. The reasoning is simple: why risk jail, a criminal record, and the stigma from illicit drugs when alcohol is legal, openly available and, most important, socially accepted. There's no family disgrace in alcohol, especially when parents keep it in the home and occasionally imbibe themselves. So what we're doing is shifting the acceptability of a sickness. Drug addiction is an unlawful sickness; alcoholism is a legal sickness. . . . We destroy ourselves and our children on the premise that a martini, or two, or three . . . are relaxants after a hectic day. We give the impression to our kids that drugs are bad, but that there's nothing wrong with drinking. . . .
>
> The . . . parent gets loaded. The child watches. The next morning the parent takes something from the medicine chest. The child watches. What the kid has learned is that alcohol is permissive and socially accepted, and that in case of stress or harmful effects, there's always something in the medicine chest.

The problem is not solved through nagging at the teen-aged drinker, however. As the staff of Family Counseling of

Kids Drink Because of Parental and Social Influences

Greater New Haven, Inc., recently reported to readers of the *New Haven Register*:

> The time to make a youngster aware of the dangers of alcohol is before it has become a way of life. Teenagers notoriously do not respond to parental preaching. A long sermon on the evils of the Devil Rum [sic] or Satan Apple Wine probably won't drive Johnny or Susie back to Kool-Aid or Pepsi-Cola. But what he or she observes in the home will have an influence, whether the parents realize it or not. . . .
>
> Adolescents who see their parents or other important adults in their lives treating the abuse of alcohol lightly, are much more apt to start drinking excessively and early themselves than those who grow up in homes where liquor is regarded realistically.

In a survey of the sophomores in five Virginia counties, the staff of a state division of alcoholic services found that almost 1,300 students indicated that student drinking was positively correlated to the cultural acceptance of alcohol and drugs, to the parent-child relationship, and also to the student's "success drive." Responding to questions concerning their awareness of the effects of alcohol, their attitudes toward intoxication, and their familiarity with drinking adults, the students indicated that more alcohol use is evident in the group which considers alcohol and intoxication as socially acceptable, normal, widespread, and harmless. "In other words," the report says, "there is more drinking among sophomores who believe that the use of alcohol is condoned by society."

And again, the survey indicates, when any form of punishment is involved, the level of daily drinking is much lower than when there is no expected punishment. Note that the survey also considers the levels of punishment in relation to the drinking sophomore: no punishment, a possibility of punishment, talking, mild punishment, severe punishment. The *mildly* punished students are the smallest portion of drinkers, while the nonpunished are the highest. This would seem to indicate that moderately drinking kids themselves expect and respect parental control more so than the heavier-drinking kids. In fact, a 15-year-old Chicago student, when asked how she felt parents should react to their kid's drinking said, "I think parents should really come down hard on them, for their own good."

That the quality of the parent-child relationship is one of the most significant factors affecting a child's potential drinking habits is also underscored by the Department of Transportation's National Highway Traffic Safety Administrations landmark study reported in Part I. When asked, "Is it the parent's responsibility to explain the use of alcoholic beverages?" 70 percent of the ARS (alcohol-related-situation) students replied affirmatively. When asked, "Should parents be more concerned with alcohol than with marijuana?" 45 percent of the kids replied *yes*. And when asked, "Should parents be tolerant if their teens drink too much?" 42 per cent of the students replied in the negative. Clearly, the drinking kids themselves see parents as guides to their drinking habits, teachers in the school of alcoholic consumption, and models for their future roles as drinkers in American society.

According to Bob Groves, executive director of the Alcohol and Drug Abuse Center of Royal Oak, Michigan, a Detroit suburb, many youngsters are drinking not just because "they're sick and tired of getting ripped off on street drugs," but also because parents accept drinking more easily than they accept drugs. "For many parents, it's a matter of life-style —they don't say much until drinking becomes a problem."

And Ken, a young Royal Oak A.A. member, added, "Some parents will tolerate alcohol, even to excess, as long as the kids stay away from drugs. And until the 18-year-old drinking law went into effect [in Michigan in 1972], these kids weren't showing up at meetings."

"Most Americans think alcohol is a recreational beverage instead of a drug," says Dr. George Maddox at Duke University. In an article in *Today's Health* (November 1970), Dr. Maddox said that most young people try to mimic adults and their ultimate outlook toward alcohol is "largely influenced by the conduct and attitude of their elders." The seemingly harmless setting of the cocktail party in the home provides a "romantic backdrop" for young people who visualize themselves as part of the group. They conclude that holding a highball glass is one of the simplest methods of edging toward adulthood.

Take a small child to a restaurant and observe how the waiter will cheerfully offer to bring a "Shirley Temple" for the child along with the regular cocktails for the adults, so that the child will think he is drinking along with the adults. This carries over into puberty when, as a teen-ager, the child finds other beverages to continue the ruse of adulthood—usually wine diluted with water at the dinner table and a "harmless" drink at the grown-up cocktail party. Dr. Maddox believes that teens drink frequently for fear of being left out of the group, and that this fear supersedes the fear of running afoul of the law or being involved in an auto accident. However, for purposes of this section of the book, it's important to remember that this fear of being part of the group doesn't apply only to peer groups—it also holds true in the home, and especially at the cocktail party, when the child is even more conscious of his "childness" and wants to be associated with the adult world more so than when he is with his own circle of friends.

Why Do Our Teen-agers Drink?

In January 1975, *Parents Magazine* reported:

Children who become accustomed to parental abuse of alcohol are learning dangerous lessons. Parents recovering from hangovers, parents moving in a circle wherein excessive drinking in bars and at cocktail parties is accepted social behavior, parents who use alcohol to escape from their problems—all may be contributing to a future drinking problem in their children.

The article quotes Dr. Bernard Heyman of Grasslands Hospital in New York State: "Of all addictive agents, two are without question physically damaging and life threatening. These are the two legal ones—alcohol and tobacco." The article also cites a Health, Education and Welfare Department study in which alcohol was related to certain cancers. It said that heavy drinking, especially in combination with heavy smoking, may be associated with "cancers of the mouth, pharynx, larynx, and esophagus and primary cancer of the liver."

In a significant study of 83 high school seniors and their perceptions of their parents' attitudes toward drinking and the parent-child relationship, Thomas J. Prendergast, Jr., M.D., and Earl S. Schaefer, Ph.D., formulated some correlations between drinking and drunkenness among middle-class high school students in a North Carolina city.

The report states: "It appears that the perception of parental control, particularly by the mother, is a critical determinant of the frequency of drinking and of drunkenness [among high school students]." Ask yourself, then, whether you or your spouse seems to exercise more control over your children. Who talks to them about drinking, if at all? How often does the family discuss drinking alcohol? Who leads the discussion? Which parent drinks the most, and to whom are your children's questions directed most often? How would you evaluate your and your spouse's stand on drinking alcoholic beverages by your teen-ager (*as perceived by your teen-ager*):

a. You don't care much.
b. You'd rather they didn't drink until legal age.
c. You forbid drinking and definitely frown on it by your kids.
d. You'll tolerate moderate drinking in the home but not outside.
e. You'll tolerate moderate drinking in and out of the home.
f. You'd react with some form of punishment if one of your children got drunk.
g. You'd react with words or a lecture, but no punishment.

Ask yourself, also, whether your own selection of what your kids would think your reaction would be jibes with what you think your spouse's reaction would be. Do the two agree? Ask your children . . . does *their* selection agree? If not, it's the time right now to sit down and have a discussion about drinking. Regardless of whether you think you have firm control over your children, it's whether *they* think you have firm control that matters as far as potential drinking problems go.

Drs. Prendergast and Schaefer conclude their study with a typology of the family in which excessive drinking by adolescents is predicted:

—a family in which the father drinks;
—a family in which the child feels loosely controlled;
—a family in which this loose control is specifically on the part of the mother;
—a family in which the child feels rejected by one parent;

—a family in which the child perceives a great deal of psychological tension between himself and the father, or between father and mother.

"The students' drinking frequency was significantly correlated with the firm-control, lax-control factor from both mother-child and father-child relationships," the report concluded. "With respect to both parents the direction of these correlations was for more drinking to be associated with lax control." This substantiates what many drinking youths themselves have told us in actual interviews.

A Harrisburg, Pennsylvania study of high school officials, students, and police authorities, confirmed the "Do as I say not as I do," adage. The kids themselves, it seems, laugh when asked about the accessibility of alcohol to underage drinkers. Their general opinion is that life moves now at a decidely different pace than it did twenty or thirty years ago, and that they have become more involved in the socioeconomic mainstream. Hence they feel more "entitled" to behave as adults than their counterparts of a generation ago. They fight wars, they vote, they're sexually as free as any teen-age group in history has been, if not more so, and there are few special issues and political problems they don't know about. One school principal stated, "The kids like to party. They see their parents party. And so they do as their parents do—get enough booze and beer to add a little life to the party."

After surveying thousands of youngsters, the same Drs. Maddox and McCall of Duke University concluded that drinking among teen-agers begins as a normal part of assuming an adult role in their immediate environments. In *The New Alcoholics: Teenagers*, a government pamphlet, Jules Saltman says, "Since adults approve of drinking and practice it freely in their presence, young people come to regard drinking as a badge of adulthood, and among boys as a sign of virility." Mr. Saltman explains that Drs. Maddox and McCall were told by teenagers that the reason they thought adults drank was mainly "for sociability and self-expression" and to "bring down their feelings of anxiety."

Another study, made by the Kentucky Department of Human Resources, showed that parents' habits are the determining factor on whether teen-agers drink. The teen-agers' first personal experience with alcohol typically happens at home at the ages of 13 or 14, the study said, and not at wild parties. The study indicated that youths in the state of Kentucky are strongly influenced by the state's 1,000,000 drinking adults and the estimated 140,000 alcoholics. Dr. Stanly Hammons, commissioner of the D.H.R., said that teen-agers who drink generally report that at least one parent is a drinker (not necessarily an abuser); among nondrinking teen-agers, it is usually reported that neither parent drinks.

According to James R. McKay, a psychiatric social worker in New Hampshire: "Regardless of the diverse opinions expressed by the adult world to teen-agers at home, in school, in church, among their peers, or through the mass media, it appears that the bulk of teen-age drinking can be understood as culturally conditioned and socially controlled behavior." Those who have studied teen-age drinking have repeatedly pointed out that, for many, drinking is linked to the passage from adolescence to manhood. For this group, part of an adult identification includes the moderate use of alcoholic beverages. If it is culturally prescribed that adult behavior includes the drinking of alcoholic beverages, then it is not surprising that teen-agers drink. It is interesting to note that one study disclosed that those students who considered themselves to be "drinkers" also saw themselves as adults.

Why Do Our Teen-agers Drink?

As H. David Archibald, executive director of the Addiction Research Foundation in Ontario, Canada, put it:

> In our response to drug abuse we have been through a series of battles; we have come out of each of these a little battered and, I hope, a lot wiser. But I am afraid we have also come out a little desensitized, complacent, and, I believe, highly vulnerable. Let me give you an example. Three years ago when we reported that almost 20 percent of our high school students had tried marijuana, parents and school officials reached the edge of panic. A few months ago when we reported that almost 80 percent of high school students drank alcohol, and many of these were drinking frequently, there was one collective yawn. Even so, there was a feeling of relief that at last youngsters in our schools had come to their senses and had come back to something we could all accept.

Lura Street Jackson, in an article in the December 1974 edition of the *General Federation Clubwoman*, cites some sociologically-induced reasons children may seek escape through alcohol. Ms. Jackson is the Drug Program Advisor for the National Institute on Drug Abuse.

> Some perceptive social critics have built a very good case that the last days of the 20th Century are a transition between two eras: we have not yet adapted to the requirements of technological society, and have lost many of the stabilizing institutions. We face a new world and yet our children are being prepared for this experience . . . by schools and learning systems designed for an earlier era when generally similar life patterns were passed from one generation to another.

When alcoholic beverages are used as part of a diet, excessive drinking and drunkenness are not common. One can find whole chapters in alcoholism books about bizarre cultures in deep jungles of South America, or a group of Tibetan tribesmen and their drinking habits, but here it is only important to understand that among such groups as Italians and Jews, where alcohol is either used primarily with food or in religious ceremonies, there is relatively little problem with alcoholism. However, among the Irish, *who seem to have to go outside the home to drink,* or who drink simply for the purpose of getting drunk, there is a very high incidence of alcoholism. In this country there has been only token use of alcohol as a food product—wine, in most cases—and we have what is considered one of the highest rates of alcoholism among free world nations.

In the America of fifty years ago, more drinking took place in public drinking establishments, but today more drinking is done at social affairs and in the home than in public, hence it is easier for a teen-ager to drink than it was a generation ago. Thus an increase in personal and community responsibility is needed, especially in the home. If excessive drinking is openly disapproved of, and pointed out whenever it occurs in proximity to the family, youngsters within that family group will grow up with a healthier respect for alcohol. Parents who make as big a deal of tolerating only *responsible* drinking in their home as, say, safe driving or sexual discretion, would be doing their children one of the biggest services of their lives. We say, "I worry when you drive with So-and-so because he gets a lot of speeding tickets and is reckless." We say, "Treat your body with respect and guard against sexual pressures until you are an adult." But do we say, "Look at that fool Mr. So-and-so, (a friend of the family) who gets himself drunk and can't function properly"?

Why Do Our Teen-agers Drink?

The Cooperative Commission on the Study of Alcoholism said in its report to the nation: "Americans prepare for participation in most adult roles; for example, teenagers are not allowed to drive without instruction from adults. Yet there is generally little preparation of young people for their imminent exposure to a drinking culture."

Finally, the role of liquor industry advertising is not a small one in determining drinking behavior from a social point of view, and it has a direct causal effect on the drinking attitudes of underaged children.

One of the surefire indicators that *anything* is on the increase is the advertising industry. We may conclude with absolute certainty that if something isn't profitable, it won't benefit from massive advertising budgets and hoopla in the mass media. If you have a new brand of blue potatoes introduced to the market and spend $1,000,000 to advertise it, those potatoes had damned well better sell like crazy for you to boost your advertising budget the following year.

Therefore, when we learn that sales of "pop wines"—the sweet-tasting 9-percent wines aimed at the youth market —have gone from 3,000,000 gallons in 1968 to more than 33,000,000 gallons in 1974 and that advertising budgets are now up around the $100,000,000 mark for these wines alone, that has to be some indication of teen-age drinking habits in the United States.

One of the most glaring manifestations of how our society encourages drinking—and specifically entices our youngsters with sweet wines and "fun" drinks—is the massive advertising campaigns financed by the distilled spirits industry.

The alcoholic beverage industry spends more than *$400,000,000* to get people to enjoy the good life that allegedly accompanies drinking alcoholic beverages. This is irrefutable evidence that alcohol is part and parcel of our society.

The trouble is that the industry makes a concerted effort to get youngsters hooked early, so as to make them regular customers later on in life. Young people are shown having a great time at the beach—along with a few cases of beer. Even the contemplative, peaceful fisherman cannot seem to enjoy his pastime without a six-pack of beer dangling over the side of his rowboat or anchored safely to a rock in the clear blue stream. One manufacturer urges us to grab all the gusto we can out of life with his beer, and another suggests that we haven't really made it in life without converting to his scotch of a certain colored label. All through this, the kids are deciding that booze is okay, because everyone is telling them it is, including T V personalities and sports heroes. But the advertising for "pop" wines does *not* tell us that, with all the sweet flavoring to make it tasty, it's 9 percent alcohol and is twice as powerful as beer.

A leading California alcoholic treatment official said recently that the liquor industry specifically aims much of its advertising at blacks and young adults. Loren Archer, director of the Office of Alcohol Program Management, told a Senate subcommittee this year in the state capitol that anyone can learn of this strategy by reading a publication called the *Liquor Handbook*, which tells which groups should become targets for marketing campaigns. The industry acts largely upon the advice in this book.

"There's nothing wrong with it [targeting blacks or other groups for its advertising]," Archer said. "It's simply in the economic self-interest of the industry. The majority of our population will be under 35 in the next five years. This is a group with the most disposable income and it is a target of the alcohol industry." Archer explained that blacks are part of the special target strategy because "the industry realizes that they increasingly will have more money to spend." He also noted that the liquor industry alone spent $157,000,000 in 1972 to advertise, and that did *not* include the beer and wine industry.

Dr. Morris Chafetz also is alarmed about the success of the "pop" wine industry among the younger set. "The sales of these strawberry, apple, and other fruit wines has increased tenfold in the past four years," he said recently. "And it's the youngsters who drink it."

Dr. Robert Niedich, Superintendent of Schools in Levittown, New York, agrees. "That stuff [sweet wines] is advertised on TV in a party atmosphere and it looks like fun. The sweet wines are almost entirely a youth market—you won't find many adults who can stomach them."

A report to the North American Congress on Alcohol and Drug Abuse in San Francisco, by Barry Peterson, Ph.D., Judith Kuriansky, and others from the New York Scientists' Committee for Public Information, stated that "The role of television advertising in promoting widespread drug abuse is an issue of grave public concern," and that because television is considered by Americans to be the most believable of all mass media, "some investigators have concluded that there is a link between the promotion of legitimate drugs and drug misuse and abuse."

(It is significant that their report did not consider alcoholic beverages because television, in its infinite wisdom and concern for public morality, has banned the advertising of distilled spirits, just as it banned cigarette advertising. Why wines and beers are not also banned remains a mystery as does the continued advertising of cigars and cigarillos.)

In a *Firing Line* television show in recent years, host William F. Buckley had as his guests Dr. Joseph Hirsh, director of the Division of Social Research and Education of the Licensed Beverage Industries, Inc., and Fr. Peter Sweisgood, counselor-in-training (at that time) for the Long Island Council on Alcoholism. Dr. Hirsh, clearly supposed to defend the sale of distilled spirits, was confronted with the fact that the H.E.W. report stated that alcohol was the "principal special victimizer,'' and the National Council on Alcoholism report stated that while 1 out of 1,000 habitual smokers dies of cancer, 1 out of 12 alcoholics dies of alcoholism. Fr. Sweisgood asked repeatedly why the labels of alcoholic beverages don't state ''Warning—May Be Habit-forming'' or ''Injurious to Your Health,'' as cigarette manufacturers have been forced to do, but no satisfactory answers were forthcoming. Fr. Sweisgood even went so far as to call the liquor distributor and the ad man the ''local pushers'' of this particular drug. ''The pusher now sees drinking in junior high school. The drinking age is getting younger all the time, and his market is growing.''

The alcoholic beverage industry, of course, will point out readily how it helps sponsor various research programs and rehabilitation efforts. Yet it doesn't seem to want to kick in its share of the cost of treating those who have become ravaged by its product. This is nowhere evidenced as strongly as in California, the state with the worst alcoholism rate in the union, where Senator Arlen Gregorio is playing St. George to the liquor industry's dragon by championing legislation that would use a small increase in taxes on alcoholic beverages to fund community alcoholism treatment and rehabilitation centers. Senator Gregorio argues:

> Most people are unaware that California has lower taxes over all on alcoholic beverages than any other large industrial state in the union which does not use the system of state liquor stores. And we derive a much lower percentage of our state budget from such taxes than does any other state which permits private off-sale of alcoholic beverages—and yet retail prices are often lower in those other comparable states.

The liquor industry argues that it is already burdened with

heavy taxes in California—yet in the 34 "license" states California ranks 17th in distilled spirits excise taxes, 33rd in wine excise taxes, and 31st in beer excise taxes. The liquor industry's lobby (a strong and rich one in the state capital) also argues that not all consumers of alcoholic beverages should have to pay for the problem of alcohol abuse by the relative minority who can't handle booze moderately. However, while this may not seem like an unreasonable position, the overall tax increases would be practically negligible to consumers, and where else are the funds to come from? California has the dubious distinction that 10 percent of its adult population has serious drinking problems (and 10 percent of *those* are teen-agers!), while 16 percent of the total population are outright alcoholics. We feel that regardless of the other 84 percent's ability to handle booze in relative moderation, the liquor industry has *some* kind of an obligation to those helpless 16 percent. Senator Gregorio polled his constituency; 58 percent favored the tax increase.

Dr. Joel Fort, a San Francisco drug-abuse expert and founder of "Fort Help," a treatment center clinic in that city, testified before the Senate subcommittee that "Alcohol is overproduced, overdistributed, overadvertised, and remarkably undertaxed." He encouraged the tax Senator Gregorio was fighting for, to the tune of two cents on a six-pack of beer, two cents on a fifth of table wine, and only six cents on a typical fifth of whiskey. But James D. Garibaldi, lobbyist for the Wine and Spirits Wholesalers and called by one newspaper "the most powerful man in Babylon," told the Senate that the sale of alcohol does not lead to alcoholism. (Quite an unbiased statement for a man whose expense report for the *month* of April 1973 was $4,066.28!) Gregorio's bill was passed with the treatment plan, and the funds allocated (reduced from $12,000,000 to $9,000,000 by Governor Reagan), but *without* the alcoholic beverage tax, which at this writing is still in committee.

The consumption of alcohol is such a deeply ingrained element of our society that entire legislatures, statewide programs, and bodies of citizens numbering in the hundreds of thousands are occupying their entire work days and personal lives toward it in some way. And in the middle of all the furor, all the psychological studies about why the kids drink, is the individual parent. He reads stories in the newspapers about kids drinking, he sees films on television of bloodied young bodies in automobile wrecks, he hears on the radio about alcohol-stimulated robberies, crime, and mayhem, and yet he never once wonders why, if *his* cocktail party got so rowdy and noisy and even a bit violent that the police had to be called, there would be no mention of it in the newspaper in the morning. Yet if his *son's* party were brought to the authorities' attention the headlines would scream:

POLICE CALLED TO
WILD TEENAGE DRINKING PARTY!

Kids Drink
"For the Effect"

At St. Mary's Hospital in Minneapolis, the only detoxification center in the state designed specifically for adolescents, drug program coordinator Jeffrey Malmquist was asked his feelings about why there is a "sizable and growing" waiting list for admission into the center. "There's just an incredible demand," he said. "We're dealing with a segment of the population that loves being intoxicated!"

A young member of the San Mateo (California) Youth Advisory Council cautions that one of the implications of drinking for the effect alone is that the drinker is shunning the responsibility of drinking intelligently. "The young people drink to escape a hopeless life," he stated. "The kids seem to believe that one of the reasons behind drug use today is that the youth of today doesn't have any self-worth. He's not looking forward to anything. We have to teach the kids to *value* themselves."

Kids Drink "For the Effect"

Dr. John Lee of Mill Valley, a prominent San Francisco Bay Area physician, has some interesting views on this subject:

When I was a kid, we'd have a few beers, you know, and getting drunk was an accident. We were afraid to get drunk, afraid of the outcome. Today, kids seem to drink with the express purpose of getting drunk. Maybe one of the reasons why kids are drinking more and harder these days is because in today's society they have no responsibility. They don't feel useful, so they get bored and try drinking, along with other "kicks." Back then, if you didn't weed the garden the vegetables wouldn't grow, and if you didn't milk the cow the cow would suffer. Also, when a kid couldn't cope with something, he could do something about it. He could run away and join the circus, or sign up as a cabin boy on a ship. He was on his own and he could find his identity. I'm not advocating that kids run away, understand, but when I was a kid we didn't have the troubles our kids have because we had working models. We could look at our parents and the other adults and follow their example. Kids nowadays don't have that. They see their dad going to work as the account executive of an ad agency, but they don't really know what he does. They don't see anything concrete, like the shoe the cobbler made, or the harvest of a farmer, or the tools of a plumber. They see their Dad going to work everyday and doing 'something' and coming home every night and having a few martinis.

In "Alcohol Abuse and Alcoholism in the Young" *(British Journal of Addiction, 1968),* Glatt and Hills state the case that the young problem drinker is distinguished from the normal adolescent drinker by his early use of alcohol for its effect.

Abnormal drinking patterns in this behavior type "seem to be an attempt to shortcut to an adult role, supplying a false feeling of omnipotence to the disturbed personality acting out his inadequacy." Of course, one doesn't have to go so deeply into psychological esoterica to conclude that a youngster who drinks for the effect of altering his reality to the point of feeling "omnipotent" will most likely be the kid who displays abnormally pronounced feelings of inferiority. Parents should note such indications early and not merely chide the child or pooh-pooh his "silly attitude."

One of the primary reasons that kids seek the effect of alcohol is a certain psychological freedom it gives them. The poor dancer, the shy wallflower, the socially awkward—all of them exist in the teen world just as surely as they do in the adult world. The boisterous life of the party who needs a few drinks before he'll start playing his guitar or dancing has his own counterpart at the teen-age party where a few drinks are needed to loosen up the gang. The insecure adolescent is one of the personality profiles that is in the gravest danger of becoming a problem drinker, experts say. A psychological dependence to smooth out the rough edges of the self-image is no different from a group of adults having to have a few cocktails before a party can really get started.

"When you're drinking," one teen-ager told us, "you get a glow on and you can suddenly play any role you want to—any role you *have* to play to go along with a particular crowd." Other kids across the country expressed their own variations on this theme, as our interviews show.

"When I'm straight I can't talk to girls right," said one Detroit teen, a high school dropout. "I can't tell them how I really feel. But I get a little drunk and the words come up right then and there when you're talking to them. It more or less brings the man out in you."

One of the problems with drinking "for the effect" is that

whatever age the child is when he starts depending psychologically on the effect of booze, that's the age he *still* is when he has overcome the problem. In other words, when a child is 14 and starts drinking to become socially more relaxed and able to cope with social pressures and anxieties, that child can still have the dependence on alcohol at 18, and after he quits drinking, if he does, *he will still be 14 years old socially.* "When a kid comes in here," says Fr. Vaughn Quinn, director of Detroit's Sacred Heart Recovery Center, "we put him through a seventeen week program and for a while everything's great. Then he goes right back into the same environment he came from and suddenly realizes he hasn't learned a damn thing in life. He's learned all his social behavior patterns while drinking, and people who do that dissolve them away as fast as they learned them. If the kid was 12 when he started drinking, that's what he is when he stops drinking. With teen-agers we're not talking about rehabilitation—we're talking about *habilitation*, from the word 'go.' "

However, when we say "for the effect," we do not necessarily refer only to relaxation. There are other effects, chiefly some form of altering reality to suit the fantasies of the drinker. In an article in *Science News*, David C. McClelland of Harvard claims many psychiatrists are in error when they state that we drink to relieve anxiety and to curb tension. He reports that we drink chiefly because we enjoy the experience it produces—the "effect"—inasmuch as the weak feel stronger, the ugly handsomer, the cowardly braver, the inhibited freer, etc. He also states that excessive drinkers usually have excessive aggressiveness and fewer inhibitions to begin with. Further, his co-researcher Sharon C. Wilsnack found that drinking enhances feelings of womanliness in females. One would assume that soon after puberty, when "womanliness" and "manliness" are just beginning to come into full bloom, methods of enhancing those feelings would be embraced wholeheartedly. If one of the methods is alcohol, sexual experimentation is inevitable.

Another reason kids turn to alcohol and its effects these days is that there is a growing nihilism on the part of this new generation. The seeds of this despair were sown during the Vietnam war, when many felt deeply that the killing was morally wrong but felt helpless to do anything about it. Demonstrations and rebellious behavior patterns became the order of the day, and ultimately this growing discontent was fed by the highly publicized collapse of political morality in the Watergate affair. Then came a new administration, and with it continuing food and energy crises, and a faltering economy featuring high unemployment, until finally we are left with a society of teenagers who don't seem to give a damn, who tack the nagging phrase "If we're around then," or "If I'm still alive then," onto every mention of a future time.

George Wald, professor of biology at Harvard and a Nobel Laureate, addressed M.I.T. in 1969. He said, "I think I know what is bothering the students. I think that what we are up against is a generation that is by no means sure it has a future."

The plain fact is that one of the aftereffects of the cold war, Vietnam, and Watergate on our youth is that they are now a generation seeking kicks more than careers, fun more than future. Add to that the tightening of drug laws and the feeling of the economic and political uncertainty of the 1970's, and you have the right set of conditions for a drinking generation. The results are visible in the stories now emanating from the nation's newspapers about the return to "normalcy" on college campuses—the resurgence of fraternities, sock hops and drinking. A University of Rhode Island study (Rhode Island is one of the four top alcoholism states in the nation) found that 102 college student unions sold alcoholic beverages in 1972, and nearly half of these so-called "wet" campuses received their licenses between 1968 and 1972. The study showed that 130 colleges not selling alcoholic beverages then were nevertheless contemplating it, 24 were actually planning a drinking facility, and 14 already had the turnover in progress. In an article in *Institutions/Volume Feeding Management*, a trade publication aimed at those businessmen who run mass food and beverage outlets, the statement was made this year that "Ideological rap sessions are on the wane; fraternity beer busts are on the rise." The article goes on to report that beer and wine are the popular drinks on campus. (The average price, incidentally, is $1.30 for a 60-ounce pitcher of beer, 46¢ for a 6.6-ounce glass of wine.) "At the State University of New York (Binghamton), wine-tasting parties introduce students to wine as a cultural and educational experience," the article states, "eliminating the need to see who can chug-a-lug a bottle of pop wine the fastest." The "nonprofit" reason for the existence of liquor being served on campus is given: "Liquor is a real social asset," one student union director says. "Students can count on finding a significant number of their fellow students available in a relaxing atmosphere. It provides the possibility of social contact with faculty and staff."

The drugs that accompanied the rebellious sixties have given way to the socially acceptable use of alcohol. An interesting version of the "drug culture fallout" theory of why kids drink is put forth by Richard Cargill, director of Pharm House, a drug-abuse treatment center in Minneapolis. The stridency of the late sixties has mostly vanished, Cargill thinks, hence "Most youths who once might have avoided alcohol because it was the 'establishment' intoxicant, no longer consider themselves part of a cohesive youth movement that [categorically] rejects the habits of their parents."

In truth, even the most adamant prohibitioners are hard put to deny the relaxing powers of alcohol. Indeed, a drink at the end of a hard day does relax the body and the mind—the only good thing there is to say about alcohol's effect on the person consuming it. Young and old alike use a drink or two as an escape from tension, and many doctors prescribe doses of alcohol for certain disorders relating to tension and anxiety. But what about boredom? When the evidence indicates that youngsters are turning to booze as an escape from boredom, shouldn't we then become worried? Are we a generation of bored people breeding a new generation of even more bored people? As the quality of life changes in the midst of urban decay and suburban sprawl, are our teen-agers turning to alcohol simply to create excitement? Are there not enough tennis courts, open fields, concerts, dances, automobile engines, books, acrylic paints or—God help us—television sets to keep the kids interested and occupied? Is there no more room for, or encouragement of, mental challenges?

Why *do* kids get bored? Do we lack goals, or do we simply not talk about them as much? Are we turning away from achievement; from the single-minded determination to reach a certain level of excellence in a sport or profession or a trade or a creative talent? Were our grandparents bored? And if not, why not? Is there something missing from our system of values that's creating this vacuum of boredom into which our kids are sucked?

Maybe things are too easy now, maybe we have finally reduced our frontiers down to the point where a genuine challenge has gone the way of the condor or the brontosaurus. Maybe there are, after all, too many of those television sets; maybe we've been grooved into a world of rote work, rote play, and rote home life. Maybe because we, as parents, seem no longer able to entertain ourselves without drinking, our kids are taking the logical shortcut that any laboratory rat would discover: quit that birth-education-work-achievement-retire-death ethic, and end it all faster by drinking sooner.

7

Kids Drink Because of Peer Pressure

I don't see hardly any of my friends anymore. They
always want to go to a bar. I spend most of my time with
my girlfriend. I went to a graduation party last June, but I
had to leave because I couldn't take it. Everybody was
looking at me kind of funny, asking me why I wasn't
drinking. I told them I was an alcoholic, but they didn't
believe it. Most young people find it difficult to believe.
They kept telling me to forget about it and have a drink.

Marty, 18, A.A. member

It is rapidly becoming a cliché that the youngsters who
insist most on preserving their individuality, who complain
most noisily about their lack of freedom and not being trusted
by their parents, are the most chronic conformists of all. They
can be seen wearing the same things, following the same sports
fads, the same cliques, using the same jargon, and doing the
"thing to do," going along with the crowd. Unfortunately,

this carries over into drinking and drug abuse, too. Peer pressure is one of the most popular responses when young teenagers are asked why they drink—not in those terms, but in "the-whole-gang-drinks-and-you're-out-of-it-if-you-don't" kind of argument.

A high school teacher in Newport News, Virginia, was told by a student, "I didn't have any friends as long as I refused to drink. Now I do, and my social life is really good." And a high school principal in Harrisburg, Pennsylvania, says:

> Kids have got to do the "in" thing. You can't be a square in a crowd at a Friday night party when the booze is passed around. The party is the name of the game. That's where youngsters spend most of their weekend time, and it's where the peer pressure is the greatest. The kid who doesn't take something to drink has a dozen of his friends all over him. It's a lot like adults act when one of the crowd is on the wagon.

The parallel is apt. Have you ever noticed how everyone feels sorry for someone who is on the wagon for a while, or cutting down his drinking for some reason or another? How there is jubilation and celebration when he resumes his old drinking habits? It may very well be a variation of the old "misery loves company" situation, wherein the person who knows his own drinking has become more excessive than he cares to admit, welcomes the similar failing of a compatriot and perhaps even looks upon it as a sympathetic relationship. The pressure on a nondrinker is as severe in adult society as it is in the underage kid in high school or junior high.

The peer group pressure aspect of teen-age drinking extends into peer group *pushing*, too. A high school girl in Fort Wayne, Indiana, equates the pressure to drink alcohol by a heavy drinking schoolmate to the pressure to buy marijuana or begin a harder drug habit. "This one guy is always trying to sell me some dope," she states, "but I tell him no every time. He always teases me and calls me super straight, and he finally told some of my friends to watch out for me because I was a narc." Then the girl laughs. "But you know, that's just plain scary, that dope stuff. At least when they pressure me just as hard to drink at a party I can have a few beers and get them off my back."

Another high school girl in the Midwest told us that the "dare" is just as in as it always was, except that nowadays it's more of a social stigma not to go along with it than before. "Bet you can't take three hits of mescalin and chug-a-lug a six-pack of beer" isn't a wildly exceptional dare around the high school circuit these days—it's a typical one.

One high school superintendent in New York City said:

> For every student we have who has never taken a drink, there are probably a dozen of his friends urging him to start drinking with them. This is probably higher than the normal suburban statistic, but that doesn't make it less significant. I'd say most of the kids in a typical senior class drink only because their friends expect them to!

Another angle of the peer pressure centers on girls. With the new sexual freedom, the pressures on girls to drink are increasing rapidly. "Boys with sex on their minds know full well about the inhibition-releasing powers of alcohol, and they're trying every way they know, short of forcing it down their throats, to get their dates high on booze," said a prominent Los Angeles youth counselor. In the Fort Wayne, Indiana, *Journal-Gazette* a high school girl reported, "I don't need [alcohol], but there is very definite pressure on me to use it, especially from the boys I go out with."

A California physician notes another interesting sociological phenomenon cropping up among today's young drinkers, especially boys. Those who are inclined to participate in *group* sports, team sports like baseball, football, basketball and hockey, are more influenced by peer pressure than the kids who are the loners, like the tennis player or the golfer. This theory seems to be supported in the following surveys:

The North Carolina survey referred to earlier showed that urban white high school seniors confirm that the primary source of pressure to drink—in a community where major religious denominations vigorously promote total abstinence—are found within the adolescent society itself. It's significant that the 12 percent of the sample who didn't drink were kids whose parents opposed drinking and whose best friends abstained also, but 89 percent of those who drank had parents who were not opposed and had two best friends who drank. The frequency of alcohol use by the teen-agers was directly related to social support of drinking among parents and best friends. The majority of nondrinkers reported experiencing pressures to drink: as many as 74 percent of those with two drinking friends, and only slightly less for those with one drinking friend. The survey concludes that "pressures to drink are widespread in the adolescent subculture and are directly related to the peer relations of the adolescent. The behavior of the adolescent's friends not only has importance in determining whether or not he will begin drinking, but also influences other behavior and attitudes about alcohol."

One of the most significant, and, to the parent, useful aspects of the National Highway Traffic Safety Administration survey discussed in Part One of this book is the "Psychological Factor Structure" portion, which profiles the personality/life-style of the drinking teen-agers, or the ARS-involved students. It shows how group-oriented these young drinkers are, and how peer pressure is a decidedly influential factor in drinking habits. Here are the definitions and the Department of Transportation's explanation of the results:

PSYCHOLOGICAL FACTOR STRUCTURE
High School

SOCIABILITY — I spend a lot of time visiting friends.

AGGRESSION — Stupidity makes me angry.
I do not like to see anyone receive bad news.

DOMINANCE — I feel confident when directing the activity of others.
I think it is better to be quiet than assertive.

CAUTIOUSNESS — I am careful about the things I do because I want to have a long and healthy life.
I like the feeling of going fast.

IMPULSIVITY — I find that I sometimes forget to 'look before I leap.'
Rarely, if ever, do I do anything reckless.

SUPPORTIVENESS OF FRIENDS — I believe in giving friends lots of help and advice.
If someone is in trouble, I try not to become involved.

NEED FOR SOCIAL RECOGNITION — When I am doing something, I often worry about what other people will think.
I will not go out of my way to behave in an approved way.

ACCEPTANCE OF SOCIAL ORDER — I believe the society we live in is pretty good the way it is.
I would make a lot of changes in the laws of this country if I could.

107

RESPECT FOR LAW — I obey the law even when I am convinced it is in need of change.

If I can get away with it, I will break any law which I think is bad.

HELPFULNESS TO OTHERS — I enjoy helping people even if I don't know them very well.

I try to get out of helping other people if I can.

SOCIAL ALIENATION — Nowadays, a person has to live pretty much for today and let tomorrow take care of itself.

It's hardly fair to bring children into the world with the way things look for the future.

You sometimes can't help wondering whether anything is worthwhile.

HOPELESSNESS — There are many people who don't know what to do with their lives.

In a society where almost everyone is out for himself, people soon come to distrust each other.

NON-INVOLVEMENT WITH PEOPLE — Letting your friends down is not so bad because you can't do good all the time for everybody.

People would be a lot better off if they could live far away from other people and never have to do anything for them.

LIBERALISTIC — Sexual behavior should be bound by mutual feelings, not by formal and legal ties.

	Police should not hesitate to use force to maintain order.
FAMILY ALIENATION	Sometimes I feel that my parents have no real understanding of what I want out of life.
	In dealing with my family, I do not believe that there really is a "generation gap."
HOSTILITY	Sometimes I feel resentful when I don't get my own way.
	I can't help getting into arguments when people disagree with me.
AUTONOMY	If I have a problem, I like to work it out alone.
	I usually try to share my problems with someone who can help me.

THE PERSONALITY/LIFE-STYLE PROFILE OF THE ARS-INVOLVED HIGH SCHOOL GROUP

When compared with the Non-Involved group, those young people tend to be a good deal more social and group-oriented. They like to be with a group of their peers in most of their social activities. In terms of their social and civic attitudes, they are more likely to be liberal and permissive and feel that their current social environment is overly restrictive and authoritarian in its attitudes towards young people.

Their involvement in drinking tends to be very much a social activity. It is actuated not so much by antisocial attitudes, but rather by their greater degree of impulsiveness and desire to experiment with new experiences. Their willingness to do this is reinforced by their greater degree of self-confidence and ability to make their own decisions about what they want to do.

With regard to their likelihood of controlling the behavior of other members of their social group, these involved high school students display no tendency toward helping or supporting their friends. In this sense, the social group, in which they participate, is probably not very commitment-oriented and most of the students are reluctant to take the lead in attempting to influence the behavior of others. This is so even in situations which are risky from the standpoint of legal difficulties or actual personal danger to members of the group.

In other words, your child is more likely to have a drinking problem if he has little respect for the law and spends most of his time in social situations, compared to the non-drinking teen-ager.

To underscore the peer group influences on teen-age drinking habits, here are comments from three fairly typical teen-age girls in California—one from the San Francisco Bay Area, two from Los Angeles. Their remarks seem to point out to parents exactly how influential a peer group is, and to show that a tendency on their children's part to "go along with the crowd" might be an indication that sound parental guidance about alcohol and its effects has been lacking.

> The first time I ever got smashed was New Year's Eve in my sophomore year of high school. We were playing this game called toss-off, where you shake dice and chug-a-lug when you lose. I was mixing my drinks and I really got drunk. I didn't drink much before that. Maybe a half-a-can of beer like in the eighth grade or something, I couldn't even drink a whole can of beer. My dad never let me drink at home until I was 18; I guess that's why I wanted to go out and try it. Most of my close friends are

loose people. Of 50 friends, I'd say 50 drink. Of all the people who are close to me I can name maybe *one* who never gets drunk—I'm serious. Most of my friends are interested in going out and having a good time, and that's a good way to do it. For awhile I was a Jesus freak and I didn't drink much and that was cool. I guess in high school we mostly drank beer and sometimes wine, in college you start to see more kids drinking vodka and tequila and other hard stuff. I never drink when I'm home alone. It's when I'm with other people that I drink. It's a nice way for everyone to get loosened up. A party doesn't really get good until everyone has had a couple of drinks. We mostly drink at parties. Usually a kid has a party when his parents aren't at home. Who wants to go to a party when the guy's parents are there? You never really relax. I guess in the last two months I've been drunk or stoned at least every weekend. Once in a while a couple of times during the week, but usually only on weekends when we all get together and party.

Sue, 19, California

I'd say about 90 percent of the senior class in our school drinks. Most of us drink beer, probably because the hard stuff is harder to get. Sometimes someone will have a bottle of bourbon and everyone will go to the parking lot at lunchtime and drink. But most of the drinking is done at parties on the weekends. We don't drink much during the week. Sometimes we'll go to a friend's house after school and have a few beers but we don't get drunk. During the summer there's more drinking. I guess it's because everyone is having parties and stuff and if you don't want to be left out, you go along with the crowd.

Cindy, 16, California

111

I guess I really started drinking when I started skiing. They drink on the bus on the way there and on the way back, and kids who don't drink don't seem to have as much fun. We noticed that right off as freshmen, so we started drinking to get with it. Boys really put the pressure on you, too. I guess most of the sex I've had was when we were smashed, mostly in cars. Weekends almost everyone gets drunk at some party. When someone's parents are away for the weekend that's when you plan a party.

Carol, 15, California

Kids Drink Because of Emotional Disturbances

This category of reasons for teen-age drinking is probably the briefest because, paradoxically, it's also probably the most complex. The phrase "emotional disturbances" seems, in the lore of alcoholism research, to be a catch-all for anything that falls outside of "parent," "peer pressure" and "for effect" groupings. However, it seems that if a child is influenced to drink by parents, if his peer group gets to him and starts him drinking, if he has to get high to enjoy the "effect" of being stronger, older, or braver, then he most likely also has some form of emotional disturbance.

But, Dr. M.M. Glatt of Great Britain claims that youngsters who become alcoholics have "a clear maladjustment" of personality and even mental illness *before* they start drinking. In Saltman's *The New Alcoholics: Teenagers*, Dr. Glatt says:

> Young alcoholics are emotionally much more disturbed than the average adult alcoholic. The early signs of de-

pendence upon alcohol develops very rapidly; alcohol increases hostility with which the young alcoholics seem to have great difficulty in coping. Frequency of amnesia, morning and solitary drinking, and prolonged drunkenness at an early age suggest some psychopathological factors in the makeup of such individuals.

Earlier we discussed drinking "for effect" yet it is precisely this drinking for effect which in extreme cases seems to indicate some kind of emotional disturbance in the young drinker. Undoubtedly personality factors and emotional troubles are at work in the drinking teen-ager, but parents should guard against leaping to the conclusion that a child is mentally ill.

After collecting data for more than thirty-seven years, University of California (Berkeley) researcher Mary Cover Jones concluded that children who become problem drinkers in later life can be identified by personality traits in junior high school. She asserts that males who become problem drinkers can be identified during adolescence as placing heavy emphasis on masculinity and manliness, while women who probably will drink a lot show themselves in junior high as depressed, self-negating, and distrustful.

Rejection of parental authority is also looked upon as an emotionally disturbed child's manifestation. Dr. C.N. Alexander associates this behavior type with "frequent drinking, excessive drinking leading to intoxication, and drinking for psychological benefits rather than for social reasons." Here, let us remember the North Carolina survey cited earlier which indicated teen-agers with relationship problems with either father or mother—seemingly emotional in origin—are the ones who tend to become the heavy drinkers.

Dr. Mitch Rosenthal, founder and director of the famous

Phoenix House centers in and around New York, says that a child using alcohol to a marked degree may be silently calling for help. "When will you stop me?" may be the cry. Dr. Rosenthal thinks drug use is a symptom of a person's unhappiness, and that "a lot of our kids are unhappy." He points out that while the average parent still considers burglaries and crimes of violence as being perpetrated by drug addicts who would do anything for a fix, nevertheless homocides, violent crimes, and accidental deaths are far more often associated with alcohol than heroin. "I'm afraid that as severe drunkenness increases among our teen-agers, we'll soon find that out," he states.

In a limited survey taken in rural Mississippi by Globetti and Windham, a significant correlation was found between problem drinkers and deviant behavior. Aside from the obvious statistics such a small survey inevitably turns up (problem drinkers are white, blue-collar family, over 16, and so on), it was found that problem drinkers scored high on tests that isolated pessimism as a behavioral attitude, and nonproblem drinkers scored high on family unity. Abstainers scored slightly lower, while problem drinkers were the lowest on the family unity scale.

Another paper, by G.L. Maddox, which was much more intelligible in its conclusions, stated succinctly that while drinking is not the cause of antisocial behavior by teen-agers, those who commit antisocial acts are more likely to drink more heavily than others.

These same antisocial acts, according to one prominent West Coast psychologist, may be the result of underlying frustrations set up by the "hypermobility" of personal and family life in recent years. Dr. Nathan Adler, of the School of Criminology of the University of California (Berkeley) Department of Psychology, states that emotional disturbances may be set up in children of highly mobile families, because one of the functions of a community is to serve as a boundary-maker:

> We say, "People like us don't do that," or "don't do such-and-such," but when one is constantly moving about at the whim of a corporation of whatever unseen master, there suddenly are no "people like us." There is always something of a moral holiday because there never seem to be limits, no boundaries set up as standards of behavior. We are always the "stranger in town" and therefore not likely to be judged by our neighbors.

> If the company can order you to Maryland one year, and to Atlanta the next and Dallas the year after that —and you're always a hand working for the boss, so to speak, there is no center of authority for the family. What the authority figure, the father, ends up as is just another interchangeable part in a total world. The source of limits, of boundaries and authority, then comes from without the family instead of from within.

It is when these emotional disturbances are set up because of underlying frustrations—a need to reaffirm masculinity, achievement stresses, identity searching, and the like—that a child seeks the outlet or the *excuse* of alcohol to release his aggressions through defiant and sometimes violent behavior. The aggression is there in most people, but when the alcohol becomes a facilitator of such underlying aggression, it softens our controls. "It lets up on the brakes," as Dr. Adler puts it. "The emotionally disturbed child doesn't drink *because* of the emotional disturbance," he asserts, "but when he is drinking these disturbances become magnified. The problem isn't the drinking, it's the drinker."

Every culture seems to institutionalize a way of "being

bad." When marijuana became a big thing with the rebellious young generation of the late sixties, it was often a way of doing just that: rebelling. Drinking a six-pack of beer is simply another way. There is no question that a child can become so emotionally upset with something, some situation or frustration, that merely the thrill of buying alcoholic beverages at an illegal age is an act of defiance. But the well-adjusted child will get over it. He will have enough sense of reward, of recognition, that he will eventually say, "Well, I've done this and now it's a bore. Now I'll go on to other things." The element of spite, while a very important ingredient, becomes a dangerous warning sign when the spite is necessary because of a continuing underlying frustration. *"And a continuing underlying frustration,"* says Dr. Adler, *"requires a continuing underlying defiance."*

The emotional disturbances which cause children—teenagers—to begin using alcohol as a way of releasing aggressions are usually brought about by a family situation which limits the routes available to a child for the achievement of gratification. In this sense the child is no different from his adult counterpart. Using alcohol to set up a fantasy which distorts the objective situation is a dangerous sign. Moody children, continually depressed children, children with a generally poor outlook on life or a "surrender" kind of problem-solving ability, are prime candidates for chronic drinking, gambling, or drug taking.

Further discussion of emotional disturbances as causes of teen-age drinking is beyond the scope of this book. The subject is too deep and complex to attempt to place it into layman's terms and derive facile generalizations. However, it is important here to differentiate between alcohol as a *symptom* and alcohol as *behavior*. Not all alcoholics are the same kind of alcoholic, and not all "problem drinkers" or excessive drinkers are the same problem drinkers and excessive drinkers. One

117

teen-ager drinks because he feels empty, a nobody who is defective in some way, and alcohol is his stimulant. Another drinks because he is escaping from problems, perhaps achievement stresses set up by a parent who wants him to become a doctor or lawyer when all he wants to do is become a mechanic. Another drinks because of too *much* responsibility—he has to deal with problems he is still too immature to handle, or worries about problems which really aren't problems at all. There are as many reasons "why" we drink as there are people who drink.

PART THREE

WHAT TO DO ABOUT IT

Were I to prescribe a rule for drinking, it should be formed upon a saying by Sir William Temple: "The first glass for myself, the second for my friends, the third for good humor, and the fourth for mine enemies."

–Joseph Addison, 1672-1719

What the Experts Say
About Alcohol Education

There are no tricks, guidelines, magic lists of questions or books which will define for you the difference between the "problem drinker," the "excessive drinker," the "social drinker," and the alcoholic. Some researchers define "problem," or "heavy" drinking as having one drink a day; some state that a problem drinker can have only one drinking "bout" a year. Some rehabilitation groups say an alcoholic doesn't have to drink at all, while others agree with Francis Anstie, a British physician of 100 years ago, who said a "moderate drinker" is one who doesn't exceed three ounces of whiskey, half a bottle of wine, or four glasses of beer a day, and those taken only with food or meals. Which youngsters will develop drinking problems is difficult to predict. As Dr. Chafetz says "We don't know why, when people get a tubercule bacillus in their lungs, some don't get active tuberculosis and some people do." Two persons of the same size and weight can sit down and drink exactly the same amount, and one will be unable to walk across the room while the other can carry his companion home without stumbling. There simply aren't any handy labels to hang on drinkers—other than whether they *appear* to be excessive—and we will gladly leave it up to the psychiatrists and psychologists and other medically trained experts to attempt to do so. The only thing parents *can* do is be aware of the problem and follow through with some sound alcohol *education*, both for themselves and for their children. The major responsibility for this education is the parents', of course, along with the responsibility for providing schooling, nourishment and medical attention.

The education of young people begins as early as one year of age, when they begin learning the meaning of ''Hot!'' in the kitchen and ''No, no!'' in the living room. Children learn both by memory and by mimicry, and it is the latter which the parents should use to teach children about drinking. In Hans Christian Andersen's tale about the emperor's new clothes, it took a child to point out that the emperor was stark naked, because a child can spot the truth, and is more apt to respond to it than the conditioned adult. So when Mom and Dad seem normal one day and ''funny'' the next, when they have their friends in for ''drinks,'' the child sees this, remembers it, and invariably associates the ''funny'' behavior with adulthood, with being ''grown up.''

And *that's* when alcohol education begins. It starts with the parents, then filters down to their children. So the first step in educating one's child may well be an examination of one's own attitudes and practices. After all, as Dr. Chafetz points out, various personal social phenomena are not going unnoticed by the young. If we were invited to someone's house for dinner and became dreadfully ill from the food and even threw up on the table, the host would be mortified. But he probably wouldn't be so upset if we came to his house and had so much to drink that we got sick or even injured on the way home. Dr. Chafetz said the same thing of restaurants: "You have no problem closing down unsanitary and unhealthful food establishments, but you take no public responsibility for establishments that serve and encourage alcohol on people who are already 'inebriated'."

Alcohol education begins with parents finding out what the experts have to say on the subject, and then teaching themselves a few hard facts about alcohol and drinking as it pertains both to their teen-agers and to themselves. Only through such knowledge will parents be able to achieve a higher level of awareness about what's going on in their children's subcultures, and some guidelines on how to deal realistically with a drinking child.

We realize that advice is cheap. But one of the chief goals of this book is to provide the interested parent with a nutshell résumé of what's happening in the world of teen-age drinking, and what the professionals have to say on the subject. Since there will eventually be as many books on the subject as "experts," we've collated only a relative handful of the leading opinions of the day, and the most popular guidelines and theories.

In talking with hundreds of American teen-agers we have found that they are almost unanimously in agreement with most experts that if we're to prevent alcohol abuse among the young, we must institute more effective education programs at the *junior high and grade school levels*. Most teen-agers will tell you that they've heard how alcohol can hurt your liver and how drinking and driving don't mix, but that seems to be the sum total of the information they have been left with by the time they are into their junior year in high school and well into the drinking patterns of their peer groups. Since studies show that the peak alcoholism and problem-drinking ages in the United States today are between 17 and 24 years old, effective abuse prevention and education programs *must* be started at an early age in order to be effective. To do this, to gain support for such programs, adults must be willing to accept the fact that our children are beginning to experiment with alcohol, and may even be consuming it regularly, before they are out of grammar school.

The first step is to understand that *information* and *education* aren't the same thing with regard to alcohol-abuse prevention. To instill into a child a responsible attitude toward drinking requires more than delivering a mild threat about the state of his liver, reeling off essentially meaningless traffic fatality statistics, or even showing films about alcoholism. On the one hand, most children—especially teen-agers— believe they are immortal. Death, old age, the illnesses ordinarily associated with adults, and the debilitating diseases associated with heavy drinking or smoking are foreign to them. It's hard to convince a teen-ager that getting drunk three times every weekend will result in severe physical damage, when he or she can run the 100-yard dash in 9.8 or bat .375 on the school baseball team. It is equally hard to convince that same youngster that he will some day be fifty-five years old, wear glasses, and weigh 100 pounds more than he does now.

Traffic fatalities seem to indicate the same thing. The Department of Transportation study showed that drinking teen-agers don't seem to be fazed in the least by statistics or deterred by stringent laws concerning drinking. "Getting caught"—just like "getting cirrhosis of the liver"—is something that happens to other people, and most of the films being shown in the nation's junior high and high schools command an attention span of about three minutes, because they are so boring and "out of it." No, we can't *scare* kids out of drinking too much; what we *can* do is use the available information to educate them not about alcohol, but about *drinking*.

The Bulletin of the National Association of Secondary

What the Experts Say About Alcohol Education

School Principals stated: *Despite the fact that most young people drink responsibly, the adult community tends to define all youthful drinking as problem drinking.* After having examined all the facts, and after finding virtually universal agreement that from 50 percent to 75 percent of all high school juniors and seniors do *not* seem to be able to handle alcohol properly or responsibly among peer groups in unsupervised situations, this statement appears to be utterly naïve. But then one looks inside the cover of this article from *The Bulletin* (Number 326, March, 1968) and finds that it is a reprint distributed by the Distilled Spirits Council of the United States, Inc. (DISCUS), the organization seemingly dedicated to persuading everyone that everything is just fine among the ranks of drinking teenagers across the land. While psychiatrists, law enforcement officials, child psychologists, social service groups, and professional counselors from agencies and private groups in all 50 states are decrying the ineffectiveness of present abuse prevention programs and trying to alert adult America about the rise in teen-age problem drinking, DISCUS continues to issue platitudinous statements and to reprint blandly reassuring articles.

The commitment to prevent alcohol problems among our youth requires some realistic admissions of past guilt on the part of adult America. In the words of Dr. Chafetz, "For far too long in this country, we have relied on simplistic lectures and moralistic finger-shaking as educational techniques in the alcohol area [and in the drug area]. Such approaches have not worked in the past and will not work in the future." That they haven't worked is all too obvious, both in the startling increase in teen-age drinking *per se*, and in the spread of teen-age drinking *problems* to even younger age groups.

At Rutgers University, in a serious research effort into adolescent drinking, clinical psychologist Dr. Robert A. Zucker has shown that alcohol education as we practice it today falls short of effective prevention. One of the chief points of his report is that best results are achieved when a child's ideals are still being formed, still in a state of flux. This appears to be most true in approximately the 11-14 age group; education programs aimed at older age groups are less effective, because for all practical purposes the "horse is out of the barn." Dr. Zucker's report emphasizes peer involvement in abuse prevention programs, because problem drinking very definitely has peer support in the 14-and-under age group.

An important point for parents to consider, when deciding upon their own involvement in alcohol abuse discussions with their children, is that the decision-making process in drinking utilizes many of the same mechanisms as decision-making processes in other socially oriented endeavors, such as driving responsibly, earning and managing money, going steady, experimenting with sex, or marrying. Education in "coping" with the everyday problems and pressures of life is just as much an effective part of alcohol education as are the hard clinical facts about the biochemical effects of the drug itself.

"Years of painful experience have taught us that we cannot hope to achieve responsible use of alcohol solely by crackdown, by law, by moralizing, or by scare tactics," says Dr. Chafetz.

There doesn't seem to be much trouble convincing adults that better education is needed, or that they should support new and more effective prevention programs. The problem is more that the parents of America don't seem to want to change their own drinking patterns to "role-model" for their children, thereby undermining concerted abuse prevention programs by their own behavior. In a statewide California survey of attitudes about alcohol problem prevention, Drs. Cahalen, Roizen, and Room of the University of California's School of Public Health and Social Research found that about 90 percent of Californians would endorse more activity on the part of federal, state, and local governments in providing treatment of those with drinking problems. The vast majority of adults considered "teaching to drink responsibly" the main approach to education of the young, rather than total abstention or "something else." The majority also agreed that "teaching to drink moderately" was a far more preferable approach in television, radio and other media campaigns to educate the young about alcohol use.

However, *implementing* the many programs suggested by the experts is another matter. The cultural aspects—the role-modeling influences—of drinking behavior are still the greatest obstacles whenever a group of adults decide to educate the young about drinking. "The things you learn best are the things you already agree with," according to Dr. Robert D. Russell of Southern Illinois University. Dr Russell, of the school's Department of Health Education, believes it is a "hard battle" to teach our kids to drink sensibly, because the majority of us really don't agree with it, and we don't agree because we seem unable to practice what we preach. He suggests four possible steps toward educating our kids about drinking sensibly:

1. Create social concern. In China, the class is responsible for the whole group. If one person is not learning the subject, it's the class's fault. Would this work in highly individualistic America, where "groupism" and "collectivism" in all forms is fundamentally abhorrent?
2. Teach kids to be adaptable, to cope with things that don't necessarily go their own way. Better yet, teach our children when to *know* when things aren't going their own way, in order to reduce the psychological shock when sudden realization hits them.
3. Teach kids problem solving, both in the home and in the school. Many parents are so overprotective of their chil-

dren that the kids cannot learn to handle their own problems. When the children become adults, they're lost souls without the *experience* of decision making. (Often high school children are fully aware of when parents are usurping the problem-solving role, and consequently an antisocial rebellion mechanism is set up in the child.)

4. Emphasize that it's the school's responsibility to reduce ignorance, and this can be done by setting up a program with a maximum of reliable facts and a minimum of preaching.

Even the experts don't agree on *exactly* which programs are the most efficacious. While they all clamor to educate youth more effectively about alcohol abuse, many have serious differences of opinion about what, exactly, constitutes a "program." For example, Kitty Rubenstahl, drug coordinator for the city schools of Raleigh, N.C., feels teaching students about dealing with their emotions would have a beneficial effect on drinking habits. "If we provide them with experiences to develop strong attitudes so they don't have to depend on drugs, then we've got a good preventive approach. We want teachers to be more responsive to students and help their self-concepts." Similarly, the nearby Wake County school system's health coordinator, Jerry Barker, is using a form of values clarification. "We need to help students form concepts and blend in values, values that relate to having a happy or healthy life. If they have these values, then drugs won't be an attractive alternative."

On the other hand, the "spank 'em and send 'em to church" school gets a boost from a survey of 5,000 young soldiers stationed in Europe conducted by Dr. Forest S. Tennant while in charge of the U.S. Army's drug abuse program in Europe. "Never before have I been involved in a study whose results turned out to be so far off from what I expected," said Dr. Tennant in 1974, while a doctoral candidate at U.C.L.A. He had assumed that the archetypal Boy Scout who earns merit badges, raises prize-winning pets, plays the bugle in the school band and is active in sports programs would be less likely to have drinking problems later in life than the "underachiever" of low economic groups. However, among 107 different activities of the young people surveyed, the only one that showed any significant correlation to problem drinking was drinking alcohol at home before the age of 15. Even more surprising, the only two activities that related to trends *away* from drug abuse were spanking and church attendance. The Associated Press reported his advice over its wire: "Spank them moderately and send them to church and don't give them anything to drink until they're over 18, and that's about all we can say."

However, in a country that separates church from school and frowns on corporal punishment, and with huge corporate interests devoted to the selling of booze, this advice may not be very helpful.

At least one nationally known child psychologist warns us not to patronize teen-agers and to avoid "panic education." Dr. Sol Gordon of the Institute for Family Research and Education of Syracuse University, while cautioning against over-reacting to the statistics indicating a significant rise in teenage alcohol abuse, warned the North American Congress conferees: "If you come across in a patronizing manner, [the teen-agers] will turn you right off, and your federally funded, super-specialized, highly visible alcohol education program will be meaningless." We have to recall, according to Dr. Gordon, that "When drug use was the 'in' crisis, we overdosed the country with an avalanche of information and misinformation about the dangers of drugs, and the more we declaimed, the more drug use spread." He contends that stating the facts "once over lightly" will do more good in alcohol education than repeating facts over and over again until the student tunes out. He suggests trying two things in our programs:

    1. Infiltrate slowly. By incorporating various aspects of alcohol education and information into a variety of school classes, such as social studies, psychology, chemistry and health or biology, the point can be repeated without arousing antagonism as a reaction. Indirect education on sensitive topics works the best, he says, "because the kind of knowledge that's self-taught is the only real kind."

    2. Distribute "Juice Use," a "hip" comic book written by Dr. Gordon himself and Roger Conant. The comic, a somewhat patronizingly "in" presentation in itself, comprises twenty pages of cartoon drawings and breezy jokes to apprise teen-agers about the dangers of alcohol abuse. The cover depicts a drunken pink elephant envisioning a striped character who analyzes his condition as "Grape Rape," and inside there are cunningly illustrated sections on alcohol and sex, hangovers, etc. There are one million copies of the comic in distribution today.

    Many teen groups around the nation say that abstention from drinking while in early teens should be played up more as a positive personality trait than as either a "goody-two-shoes" virtue or as a "freaky" anomaly in a person's peer-group behavior. Some teen-agers have had "heart-to-hearts" with their younger sisters or brothers about not drinking when they get into junior high or high school, but oddly these same teen-agers indicate that they feel another young person is "weird" when he won't even taste a drink, especially when he's never tried it before. When questioned about this, most rational young people will reconsider this latter attitude rather than adjust the main thrust of their serious talk with a younger sibling.

    The executive director of an alcoholism council in Illinois, Jack Callaghan, sees peer group pressure as such a strong factor in teen-age alcohol abuse that he urges kids who do not drink to be more strident about it. "There are a lot of people who don't drink," he states, "and since posters and slogans don't seem to work, why not these people who don't drink themselves?" The logic is valid: if peer group pressure is so strong, why not turn it around to exert pressure on teens *not* to drink? Why couldn't three or four exceptionally strong-willed youngsters who don't drink exert as strong an influence on their peers as their drinking peers seem to exert on them?

Believable, effective alcohol abuse programs are needed. If we must educate our youth in driving responsibly before putting them behind the wheel of a car; if we must educate our youth about conception, pregnancy, and birth control before they burst forth at the height of their biological urgency; if we must teach our children love instead of hate, peace instead of war, and compassion instead of apathy, then it is painfully obvious that we must educate these same youngsters about alcohol abuse and its implications before we start selling them booze.

There are two important keys to doing it properly. One of these is to find the right people to conduct and implement the programs in the first place. In the words of one San Mateo 16-year-old, "Yeah, we do need more information about it without all the hysterics, but who's going to believe some creep who tries to tell me how *I* should act at a party?" The young are very perceptive. As more than one expert has said, they will see through hypocrisy faster than anyone, and if an instructor or parent has a hang-up about alcohol, the youngster will turn him off before he even gets his first point across. As one division director of the National Council on Alcoholism puts it: "The key is not so much *how* to teach about alcoholism, but *who* [teaches]."

The second important facet in an effective program is

what Dr. Cahalan at Berkeley calls the "scapegoating or deflection phenomenon," that is, the tendency to show enthusiasm for programs which have no immediate restrictive effects on ourselves, and then hamper programs which would cut down on our own freedom to drink or cause us to reflect more seriously about our own drinking habits.

Perhaps Polonius was speaking not to his son, but to all parents: *To thine own self be true, and it must follow, as the night the day, thou canst not then be false to any man.*

10

Some Programs That Seem to Be Working

"If you were walking down the street and saw a pill on the ground, would you stop and pick it up and swallow it?" The speaker is a handsome young man in his twenties named Bob Barnecut, an "alcohol educator" with the Alcohol Information Committee of Marin County, California.

"No!" The resounding chorus is from a group of fourth-graders at a local school, raptly participating in an Alcohol Education Program session cosponsored by the county schools. The session goes quickly and the individual responses and collective participation of the kids is almost incredible. Barnecut talks easily, intelligently, and his rapport with the kids is enviable. He touches on virtually every aspect of alcohol and drinking, and best of all, the kids *get it*. Especially when he attacks liquor advertising.

"Can you really go to the head of the class by drinking bourbon of a certain color label?"

"NO!"

"Is the best thing about Canada really the whiskey they make?"

"NO!"

"If you drink [a certain brand of wine] will you really be more popular with your friends?"

"NO!"

Barnecut goes on, warning against the insidious effectiveness of advertising, and the kids are enjoying themselves. He mentions a man walking around with a nine-hundred-pound bear, and the kids name the beer sponsor. He mentions the bull, and the kids name the malt liquor. He mentions the team of "cute" horses, and the kids name the corporation. He even mentions an old grandma doing a wheelie on a motorcycle, and the kids cry out the name of the "pop" wine advertiser. Then he mentions that this particular TV ad hasn't appeared for almost two years.

Programs like this one are beginning to be developed and tested, and one of the most important things we can do right now is to take a serious look at them and determine which ones are working. As one New York City educational director told us, "I'm so sick of guidelines and guidelines and guidelines from this organization and that organization I could go crazy. When are they going to realize that the kids are drinking *now*, and that their guidelines are more for getting new grants than for reducing teen-age alcoholism!"

The program for which Bob Barnecut works is one example of a good, practical program that is having a positive effect on pre-junior-high youngsters. The program is essentially simple. The "alcohol educator" raps with the kids and bombs all the myths about drinking in terms they can understand. He asks, for example, whether the kids *really* believe any problems will be solved by getting drunk, and by way of analogy he relates the story of a man getting two flat tires and having only one spare. The man goes to a bar and has a few drinks, and when he comes back what's happened to his problem? The kids shout out the answer. He tells how wonderful the world would be if drinking *really* made everyone happy, and the kids hear him. He asks whether, if he gave all the kids a glass of beer, they'd all look grown-up. He asks them to name various alcoholic beverages, and the kids call out dozens. He asks why people drink and invariably the kids shout "To get drunk!" At this point he emphasizes that the only *valid* reason to drink is to relax, and even then only in moderation.

The single thing that makes the biggest impression, however, is always a poster, published, to their credit, by Seagram's Distillers, It is a handwriting display of a person who, sober, writes the statement "I can drive when I drink," and then writes it again after taking two drinks, then four, and so on until, after seven drinks, the person finally writes the sentence in such ludicrously illegible fashion that it's obvious the person would kill someone if he attempted to drive a car. The exhibit strikes a chord with the students, and they exclaim loudly, often doubting its veracity. The "educator" explains the poster and the message hits home, hopefully with the same lasting effectiveness as the Annie Greensprings commercial.

"We're reluctant to join the National Council on Alcoholism or other groups interested in our program," says Helane Anderson of the Alcohol Information Committee of California's Marin County. "We'd be afraid of being swallowed up and not being able to do what we want. Many of those groups want to get grants or federal funding to make studies and find out 'what's being taught in the schools.' Well, we *know* what's being taught—nothing."

Barnecut agrees. "A lot of so-called programs consist of mimeographing some trite information, 'facts about alcohol,' throwing in a few statistics about how dangerous it is to drive while drinking, and then sending it all home with the kids after school. It rarely gets read, and if it is, it's then thrown away and soon forgotten."

The difference between effectiveness and a mammoth waste of time and money seems to be that a program shouldn't necessarily be *against* drinking as much as it should be *for* responsible drinking. Given alcohol as a fact of life in 1970s America—like taxes and ulcers—the name of the game seems to be learning to live with it and not letting it destroy your work, your enjoyment, your family, or your life.

"We teach the kids to make up their minds beforehand *how* they're going to drink," Barnecut says. "We want them to realize what alcohol really is and that the decision to use it must be an intelligent one."

"The significant thing," adds Ms. Anderson, "is that the success of a program often depends on the preparation of the regular teachers. They must decide exactly what *their* attitude toward alcohol is, and know what's going on. A lot of them know about A.A., and that's about it. Nothing about Alateen, Crisis Centers, A.S.A.P. programs and all the rest of it. They're often very uncomfortable talking to the kids about alcohol."

Two dedicated North Carolina men have developed a six-week course in alcohol decision-making. The course is given in the sixth grade and after experimental tryouts in a few elementary and middle schools, it seems to be having a markedly beneficial effect on the decision-making abilities and confidence of young students.

Marvin Aycock, a coordinator in the state's alcoholism program, and Pete Roberts, a counselor in a local mental health center serving Stanly and Anson counties, designed their "training in living education" program after deciding that the ability to make a decision is a learned one. Their innovative course, given in conjunction with a regular alcoholism and drug-abuse program in the public school system, consists of participatory class discussions, small task groups, roleplaying, word-association exercises, lectures, and films. Each class selects a steering committee from its members, and the committee helps provide ideas for class projects and role playing sessions. This stimulates group involvement and helps the students to polarize their views on various aspects of alcohol use and abuse.

According to Aycock and Roberts, by examining and going through the decision-making process analyzed and described in the course, a child can overcome the natural curiosity about "forbidden fruit." Simple information about alcohol and what it does to the body, while educational, often piques interest in a child and sets up a kind of determination to test the substance himself. The North Carolina course apparently gets the child to perceive beyond the first-stage physical effects of a harmful substance—in this case, alcohol—and to acknowledge the existence of a more profound and long-lasting effect on his or her entire life. Further, Aycock and Roberts state, because the inability to make decisions can cause a person to lose control of his life and lose the respect of friends and relatives, the improvement of the ability to make responsible decisions lessens the desire to escape harsh reality through alcohol. The independence a person gains through confidence in his ability to make important decisions has a freeing effect on the psyche, and because escapism, or "flight from fear," is one of the underlying psychological reasons for drinking heavily, this independence reduces drastically the need for alcohol or other mind-altering drugs.

Most persons involved with the North Carolina course are pleased with the results, the state's Department of Human Resources reports. After evaluating the course in first-day and last-day testing, it has been determined that the sixth-graders' ability to make decisions has been highly developed at the end of the six weeks. Increased group involvement in activities and a confidence in overall scholastic and social achievement have been noted by evaluators of the course, and Aycock states that educators "are sharing in the learning experience along with the children," and that each new class develops new techniques and ideas that are usable in subsequent classes. A concerted program *with a specific structure* seems to work far better than a vague, mysterious recitation of facts and horror stories about traffic accidents.

If there is a Jaycees chapter in your home town, you might give them a call to see whether they have a program on teen-age drinking, or at least to get some literature. The Jaycees' newly conceived Operation THRESHOLD is an alcohol education program that is doing exceptional work in responsible drinking/youth action programs. The chief mission of Operation THRESHOLD is to *prevent* alcohol abuse. "Treating only the casualties of alcoholism will never eradicate the disease," said Joseph S. Dolan, Operation THRESHOLD's program manager, in a recent speech. "We want to focus this nation's attention on prevention, to stop having to put out forest fires and get back to the tinderbox." The organization will provide interested parents with very good material on responsible drinking guidelines and other action information without coming on like a temperance group. Contact Operation THRESHOLD, U.S. Jaycees, Box 7, Tulsa, Oklahoma 74102.

The state of Illinois made an elaborate study of the status of alcohol abuse education in the school system and came up with some interesting conclusions. Directed by Walter H. Gregg, Ed.D., and Dorothy J. Clapper, Ph.D., the 4,000 teacher-and-principal study concluded:

—that no school or school system alone should assume responsibility for developing a comprehensive program, but that a school-community coordinated effort is essential if a program is to embrace not only instructional components but also assistive measures for counseling, health services and rehabilitation.

—involvement of parents in any program strengthens it and enables it to meet students' needs more easily; this involvement by parents needn't be a stumbling block to getting a program off the ground, either, because opposition to alcohol abuse programs is practically nonexistent. P.T.A. groups are the logical choice for coordinated involvement.

—alcohol abuse education should be integrated into the total curriculum, with opportunities available in social studies, science, language arts and physical education. It is "doubtful" whether alcohol-abuse education can or should be carried out as a separate or special subject in the curriculum of elementary, junior or senior high schools.

—instructional approaches should focus on *a*ffective education; teachers at all grade levels agreed that the most useful methods involve students in the study of real-life problems through decision-making experiences.

—teachers should be specifically trained, during their own education, for alcohol-abuse instruction, and the means most commonly reported by the teachers in the survey was through a portion of a college health course. As always, credibility is heightened by knowledgeability, and in alcohol abuse education, credibility is 99 percent of effectiveness.

—schools should utilize community resources to the fullest, taking advantage of service groups, lecturers, local planning groups and committees, etc.

—informal small-group activities, self-directed, are effective in the personal problem-solving educational process;

peer groups and storefront agencies are highly efficacious in getting teen-agers to involve themselves in constructive endeavors.

The University of Massachusetts, long recognized as a "hotbed" of student drinking activities throughout the western portion of the state, several years ago instituted a Room to Move program to deal with rising alcoholism on campus. Room to Move is a drug drop-in type of center which offers counseling for U-Mass. students and works closely with health officials in trying to put together a national model for other schools with similar campus drinking problems. According to E.T. Mellor, who coordinates the Room to Move education team, the operation takes a "collaboration approach" to pull together various viewpoints from all segments of the campus community to formulate twenty-four-hour hotlines, workshops and seminars, and one-on-one group counseling and spiritual alternatives. Largely as a result of this group's work, and from a conference hosted by the school's Health Services Department, a three-year proposal for a comprehensive U-Mass community alcohol action program has been devised. The program intends not only to meet the needs of students on campus, according to Dr. David Kraft, staff psychiatrist, but also to reach out to the surrounding community. He feels it is imperative to go into the elementary school level so that "some youngsters will be able to figure out why Daddy comes home one night and beats up Mommy and then brings her roses the next night." One panel session reported that an intensive six-week one-on-one counseling program at Rutland Heights Hospital had a 25 percent success rate in rehabilitating alcoholics, and that a similar technique perhaps could be instituted as part of campus service.

Similarly, the Massachusetts State Division of Alcoholism and the Massachusetts Council on Alcoholism (re-

member, Massachusetts is the heaviest drinking state) combined to conduct an "Alcohol Awareness Week," the purpose
of which was to educate the public about alcohol as a drug and
alcoholism as a treatable illness.

And in Stony Point, New York, a nonprofit educational
organization called "Drink Watchers" is using slogans like
"Hold the Line at Feeling Fine" to help educate teen-agers to
the proper way to drink. They use a connoisseurship program
to help kids learn the nuances of various wines and liquors and
to teach them to respect each type. Their newsletter can be
ordered from Box 245, Stony Point, N.Y. 10980.

A young petty officer in the U.S. Navy Fleet Weather
Facility in Suitland, Md., has developed an admirable approach to drug and alcohol education for Navy dependents in
the 11-16 age group. Aerographer's Mate Second Class
Michael Bailey has developed a first-of-its-kind series of
workshops for military children in which he and four other
sailors write, produce and act out skits in an informal setting
while the kids sit on the floor to watch the show. The skits,
which include slides, music, posters and back-lighting, are
aimed at presenting specific facts about drugs and letting the
kids draw their own conclusions. Each child fills out his own
name tag, pairs off with someone he or she has never met
before, and exchanges some personal information about
himself—a technique which effectively breaks the ice and gets
the kids to relax almost immediately.

Ordinarily, Bailey begins the discussion with a story
called "Alligator River," a tale he made up about a group of
five people, one of whom is trying to get across the alligator-
infested river to visit a lover. After the story, the children
vocally rank the cast in order of strength of character, morality, etc. In this way, each kid can see what criteria the others
use to judge people. The aim of the whole session is to make

each child aware of how his own values compare with those of his peers.

Another skit, "Chocolate Bust," is designed to show the children a typical scene involving a buyer and a purchaser of illegal commodities—in this case, chocolate. The skit reflects the feelings a child has about wanting something desperately but having to weigh the pros and cons of getting it in an underhanded way. A third skit explores parent-child communication, with two adults playing the role of children caught using marijuana. The actors portray parents and children with the traditional roles reversed to underline the two-sides-to-every-story concept. In this skit, the youngsters learn more about what their parents actually experience when children abuse drugs.

"The response and participation of the youngsters attending the workshops has been excellent," Bailey reported. "We take this type of approach because we want to present the classes with factual material and let the children make their own judgments about drugs." Because the topic of alcoholism among young people and teen-age drinking in general has become the number-one subject in drug abuse discussions, Bailey and his team produced a play—*Lady on the Rocks*, by Elizabeth Blake—which depicts the problems of a drinking mother and her effect on her family. The play workshop has been so successful that other navy commands in the Washington, D.C. area have requested a performance, and Bailey and his group now offer to perform their skits for any commands that ask for them. The effectiveness of getting across salient points about drug use and abuse to children—even facts which they've been hearing over and over to the point of boredom—appears to be very high when presented in a nonlecture, non-moralizing manner.

Bailey, who is working on his master's degree in Communications at the International University of Communications, sums up their conclusions: "After hours of research and study and the experience we've now had, I know that one statement can form the basis of our whole program: the individual's value system and basic life commitments are the best deterrents to drug abuse.''

Although it's too early to determine actual effectiveness of the total project, Montana has developed for fiscal 1975 an inch-thick master plan for a statewide alcohol abuse and alcoholism prevention, treatment, and rehabilitation system, prepared by the Montana Department of Health and Environmental Sciences. The plan, ambitious in scope and somewhat bureaucratic in its language and presentation, calls for a significant step-up in community action programs along with governmental agency support. The plan will develop special community task forces in pilot projects; establish formal alcoholism education programs at the secondary school level along with value-clarification programs organized on the elementary school level; assist institutions of higher learning in developing curricula for the lower schools; assist in parent training and program implementation forums; develop effective mass media techniques, including two radio announcements disseminated to forty-eight Montana radio stations, with follow-up campaigns, and the adoption of a series of television spots; to publish and distribute pamphlets, news articles and other literature on a regular basis.

This particular program certainly is similar to what dozens of other states are beginning to develop, but its scope and depth of study are worth mentioning simply because there seem to be too many states still in the dark ages as far as alcohol education is concerned. We contacted the directors of the departments of health in all fifty states in an effort to collate available research and published data on a state-by-state basis, but received reply letters from only twenty five. Of these, some, such as New York State, are so bound up by bureaucracy and interagency rivalry that getting further information from anything above the local community level is a frustrating effort, at best. Some officials, such as Lois M. Stiglmeier, Ed.C., coordinator of Prevention Education for the New York State Division of Alcoholism, will state only, "We hear much about 'teen-age alcoholism' yet the surveys tend to be weak in both validity and reliability. I would caution anyone to be most skeptical of these findings."

Other states, such as Georgia, will acknowledge that there is a problem in developing hard facts and effective programs for teen-age drinking and will tell you of present plans to research and develop statewide programs. Some, like Pennsylvania, will send you a mimeographed letter saying "Sorry!" and announce that your request has been "processed" and that "at present we do not have the specific information you need."

Some, like Massachusetts, Michigan, California and Illinois, will send you reams of useful information and names of responsible persons to interview, and will offer to assist you in your research. And, finally, a handful of states will kindly let you purchase their pamphlets or send you a copy of their latest research reports as long as you forward the cash first.

Michigan has sponsored a youth peer-to-peer program which could be the model for similarly chartered groups in other states or in individual counties. The youth group is called SMASH, a humorous acronym for Students of Michigan Attaining Safer Highways. It was conceived and organized by Wendy Menard, who got the idea after attending a National Safety Group convention in Scottsdale, Arizona. The whole purpose of SMASH, which is cosponsored by the Michigan Department of Public Health and the Office of Highway Safety Planning of the State Police, is "young people trying to help young people."

The program is successful in getting teen-agers active in

doing things concerning highway safety and drinking, and in educational efforts about alcohol itself. They sponsor annual drinking-and-driving conferences; send delegates to national or regional conventions and seminars; provide speakers and lecturers; disseminate information on traffic safety and drinking to whomever requests it; promote seat belt use, lower speed laws, bicycle, motorcycle and pedestrian safety, and vehicle inspection standards; and generally focus on the problems of drinking drivers. Ms. Menard believes adults cannot successfully tell a teen-ager to surrender the car keys after too many beers, so she gets other teens to do it.

"SMASH works through the high schools of the state to promote an awareness of our traffic safety problems here in Michigan," she states. "A major thrust for us is increased personal responsibility, which translates to the community at large."

High schools that join SMASH are asked to provide two students—a chairman and vice-chairman—to represent a local SMASH group and to serve as delegates from their school on the regional level. SMASH has divided the state into seventeen geographic areas, each of which reports to a regional representative for community and civic action projects. After a SMASH student graduates from high school, he becomes a member-at-large until the age of 25.

The program appears to be yet another successful attempt at getting young people *involved* in alcohol education. Placing responsibility for individual action in the hands of those to be educated is not a new concept, but far too few state organizations seem willing to abdicate total control and bureaucratic featherbedding, and to actually get a program off the ground and working in which the kids themselves participate.

Last, the alternatives theory is gaining momentum among drug-abuse educators around the nation, primarily because it seems to offer viable alternatives to drug abuse without either candy-coating or doom-saying. Advocates of the alternatives theory state that taking drugs, for whatever reasons, inevitably includes the need to escape boredom, alienation, pain, fear, frustration and meaninglessness. "People take drugs simply because they need to feel better," one alternatives program director said.

According to the theory, the "alternative" is not just another word for "substitute," but instead a constructive *attitude*, value, orientation, life-style, or pursuit which can prevent the *need* for drugs as an escape medium. Under the alternatives program, the key word is *satisfaction*—if a young person is satisfied with himself or herself, the dependency on drugs—especially alcohol—to alter reality is greatly diminished. Why alter a satisfying state? Why must reality be changed if it is a happy, contented reality?

The alternatives proponents acknowledge the popular argument that only massive cultural, sociological and economic/political changes in our society can minimize the *cause* of drug abuse. But although they agree with the long-range merit of this argument, they point out that *immediate* action is still required "under the conditions that are likely to remain relatively stable in the near future."

In short, the alternatives theory hypothesizes that people will stop taking drugs if they find something better to do, something more satisfying and meaningful in their lives. Here, in tabular form, is a capsule survey of drug-abuse motives, needs, and aspirations associated with alcohol use, and corresponding alternatives to using alcohol to achieve them. (The table excludes psychedelics, amphetamines, over-the-counter drugs, *cannabis*, and similar drugs.)

PHYSICAL
physical relaxation   relaxation exercises; hatha yoga

SENSORY
enhancement of
sexual experience

sensory awareness training;
massage; responsible sexuality
(e.g., possible education in non-
coital sexuality for adolescents)

EMOTIONAL
psychological escape
or release from
emotional agony

individual counseling

reduction of
normal tension

group psychotherapy

emotional relaxation
desire for privacy,
aloneness

special therapeutic techniques
values clarification education

intensification of
personal courage

values clarification

increase in
self-esteem

emotional awareness exercises,
such as body language,
self-awareness workshops

INTERPERSONAL
peer recognition and
acceptance

alternate peer groups;
empathetic group experiences
in peer-group processes
(encounter groups)

relaxation of inter-
personal inhibitions

competent group psychotherapy

escape/release from
family difficulties
or alienation

development of caring, personal
responsibility, confidence
and trust

establishment of
feeling of
"community"—belong-
ing with specific
reference groups

psychodrama; group activities
such as 4H, scouting, church
groups; family life education

MENTAL-INTELLECTUAL

reduction of boredom	hobbies and games; challenging pursuits such as chess, sports, etc.
curiosity	intellectual excitement through reading and discussion

CREATIVE-AESTHETIC

increased enjoyment of artistic productions	non-graded instruction in art appreciation, music, drama, etc.; creative hobbies such as photography, cooking, gardening

EXPERIENTIAL

desire for "pure pleasure," fun, recreation	self-generated play experience
nonspecific changes in consciousness, such as a "high" for its own sake	biofeedback training
engagement; the need for momentary total involvement	"mind-tripping," expertly conducted hypnosis

SOCIAL-POLITICAL

overcoming discouragement or desperation with social-political future	nonpartisan lobbying; running for office and other political activity

PHILOSOPHICAL

creation or change in values or philosophic lifestyle	reading philosophical literature
overcoming frustration from lack of meaningful vocation	values clarification procedures; metaphysical thought; exposure to committed individuals

MISCELLANEOUS

need for risk-taking, danger	sky-diving, SCUBA diving, hang-gliding, etc.
need for adventure, exploring	survival training; backpacking
"What else is there to do?"	exploring new physical environments; flying, soaring, sailing, camping in wilderness, etc.

In the alternatives theory, the information derived from nonusers in developing a program is as important as the information from the users. For example, in a survey of 800 students in a suburban high school in the San Francisco Bay Area, the 400 or so nonusers were asked the question: "What has been the biggest deterrent to using drugs?" The responses showed researchers that almost 40 percent of the students had "no need" and "my life is happy and fine" as their reasons, and another 22.4 percent placed physical or mental health and athletics as their reasons. Others included "brains" or good judgment, fear of the unknown, observation of drug takers, respect for the judgment of parents, *peer pressure against it*, and fear of addiction.

Alternatives theorists say their results with pilot programs and test procedures show a consistency with suggestions that legal constraints and scare tactics in education are only very limited in effectiveness. They say that, while tightly controlled research of clinical, observational, and statistical results is only just beginning, early results with alternatives programs encourage their continued development. Interested communities, schools, or educators are urged to contact the National Institute on Drug Abuse for a hefty resource book entitled "Alternative Pursuits for America's *3rd* Century." A small pamphlet entitled "Alternatives to Drug Abuse: Steps Toward Prevention,"

149

prepared by Allen Y. Cohen, director of the Institute for Drug Abuse Education and Research of the John F. Kennedy University, is available from the National Clearinghouse for Drug Abuse Information. It is an excellent introduction into what appears to be the new wave of alcohol and drug abuse prevention education and treatment techniques for the coming decade.

Perhaps *you* should send for these free publications for your community leaders and school principals. It may be the start of a whole new shift in the alcoholism and problem-drinking patterns among the young people in your own community.

11

The Role of
the Mass Media

Why can the Attorney General of the United States force tobacco manufacturers to place a warning on their cigarette
packages and ban their advertising from radio and TV, while
seemingly unable—or unwilling—to force the distilled spirits
people to do likewise? The answer is simply that the alcohol
lobby in Washington is richer and stronger than the tobacco
lobby and the government gains more tax money from the sale
of alcohol than it does from cigarettes. The effect the advertising industry is having today upon young consumers is becoming a cliché, and more and more advertising dollars have been
diverted from magazines and radio to television and outdoor
billboards, especially by the wine and beer industries. Hence,
more and more sales messages are reaching more and more
youngsters.

However, stronger use of television as an *anti-
alcohol*-abuse medium is currently being made, and by the
time this book is published the dollars spent on public service

television broadcasting of antidrunkenness advertising will have reached an all-time high. Such groups as the government's National Institute for Alcohol Abuse and Alcoholism and the National Council on Alcoholism have developed highly memorable ten- and thirty-second cartoon commercials shown on prime time, and even Alcoholics Anonymous, historically a low-profile organization, is creating television commercials of its own.

The television industry itself is recognizing the problem, and a rash of alcoholism-oriented productions can be anticipated in the coming months. Obviously, producers of television series and movies-for-TV are in the business of entertainment, not evangelism, and consequently much of what they are doing is profit-oriented to attract sponsors, not converts. However, they do deserve credit for inserting some kind of moral lesson into their productions. The theme of alcoholism, once a taboo on America's airwaves, is now being handled honestly and with sometimes shockingly straightforward treatment. A recent example was the series *Good Times*, which aired a segment on December 10, 1974, repeated in the spring of 1975, showing a teen-age cousin of the Evanses, visiting for Christmas, taking surreptitious nips from a bottle in the family bathroom throughout the show. In the end, the child passes out in an alcoholic stupor, while her father echoes the same old stupidity and naïveté: ''Thank God—for a minute there I thought she was on drugs!''

Another popular show that had the courage to treat the problem in a forthright manner was *Lucas Tanner*, which also used a teen-age drunk as its subject on a late 1974 show, repeated in the spring of 1975. This show, unlike the *Good Times* show, wasn't played for laughs. The *Lucas Tanner* show hired Dr. William Rader, a prominent L.A. alcoholism psychiatrist, as its technical advisor; its script had some hard pills for parents to swallow.

The program depicted a bright teen-ager from a good family who starts cutting classes. His school work drops and his grades fall. His teacher suspects that something is wrong, and after observing more closely, finally catches the boy in the men's room with a pint bottle of vodka. Tanner's first reaction is totally wrong. He reproaches the boy, accusing him of problem drinking, and in so doing completely turns him off. The boy, who is desperately searching for help underneath his outwardly defensive conduct, denies he's been drinking and begins avoiding Tanner, who finally seeks advice from a member of A.A. and goes to see a psychiatrist—Dr. Rader, portrayed by a professional actor. The doctor gives Tanner the best but most difficult of all advice to accept: do nothing. Absolutely nothing.

Tanner can't accept it. As a dedicated teacher, he *must* do something! He organizes an assembly at which a teen-age alcoholic speaks, hoping the boy will get the message; instead, the boy's resentment severs all lines of communication. The kid keeps drinking, and when Tanner finally advises the parents on what's happening, the father—drink in hand—refuses to believe his son has a problem. The mother has noticed some "hints" of erratic behavior, some classic signs of the problem drinker, but has been afraid to bring it up to her sports-oriented super-*macho* husband.

Finally, after a near-accident at a drinking party, the boy goes to Tanner's home for help. He sobers the boy up, and, of course, the kid once again shuns Tanner and refuses to acknowledge his own problem. In a climactic scene during which Tanner finally understands and tries to get across to the boy's parents that they cannot *make* him quit drinking, the boy staggers in drunk and flaunts his drunkenness at his shocked parents. Tanner ultimately does the most difficult thing, yet the only proper thing to do, according to many professional psychiatrists: on the premise that the boy must make the decision to help himself, must take the first step by admitting he has a problem and asking for help, Tanner turns his back on him and walks out, but not before explaining to the kid that they'll do everything possible to help him once he makes up his own mind. As Tanner leaves, the kid pours himself a drink, fights with his conscience, and puts the drink down. He has taken the first step to recovery.

Another show, which had a high rating impact earlier in 1975 and embraced the same treatment/rehabilitation theme, was the original television film, *Sara T.—Portrait of a Teenage Alcoholic*, competently written by Richard and Esther Shapiro. This film also used Dr. Rader for technical advice, and it states the same lesson for parents to consider and to learn.

Sara T. is a young girl in a new school, the product of a broken marriage now living with her mother and stepfather. He is the typical upwardly mobile executive; the mother is the socially active career housewife. Withdrawn and shy, Sara drinks at a party to relax, becomes accepted by her friends, and finally goes steady with a clean-cut athlete. She does the typical things for a teen-ager with a drinking problem in her socioeconomic group: she steals money from her mother's purse; she hides vodka and cherry soda in her room; she empties glasses after an adult party; she gets older kids to buy her stuff in the liquor store. When her drinking problem ultimately comes out into the open, everyone blames everything else: the father has guilt feelings because he never amounted to anything; the stepfather thinks he didn't "relate" to the child's problems; the mother thinks it's the boyfriend's or the school's fault; Sara T. herself wants help but thinks someone has to bring help *to her*, instead of vice versa. The climactic scene in this production is Sara T., drunk, offering her body to a group of celebrating seniors for some booze, then running off in a severe alcoholic depression on her boyfriend's horse which, when hit by a car, has to be shot. Afterward, in the hospital with the psychiatrist present, after all the clichés have been uttered ("Let's put this all behind us, Sara dear, and forget it ever happened. . ."), Sara herself admits she's an alcoholic and turns to the doctor and two young A.A. member friends for help.

The psychology of dealing with a drinking child will be explored later. The important thing is that finally television is facing the problem and—commercial considerations or no —presenting some useful information to the parents of America. With almost 500,000 real alcoholics today between the ages of 10 and 19, perhaps parents will watch these shows whenever possible and encourage their children to watch them also. WJBK-TV in Detroit, for example, surveyed high school students, found alcohol to be the number one drug choice, and spotlighted the findings in one of its continuing series, *Can We Win Against Drugs?* Milwaukee's WITI-TV launched a concerted drive against alcoholism with a thirteen-week series on such subjects as "Alcoholism and Youth," "Alcohol and Driving" and a ninety-minute special, *Is There Life After Alcohol?* WOUB-TV in Ohio is scheduling a "newswatch" series of special reports on teen-age alcoholism. The five-part series will focus on the drinking practices and attitudes prevalent in today's society. In Toledo, WSPD-TV received the top award from the Ohio Associated Press Broadcasters Association for a series on alcoholism during which the station fought the lowering of the legal drinking age to 18. KNXT-TV in Los Angeles broadcast a show called *The Young Alcoholics* and received such an overwhelmingly positive response that it reruns the show, or one similar to it, periodically. And Art Cole, in the Los Angeles area, reported to us that after the

Sara T. show ran for the first time, the local A.A. office had more than 400 telephone calls *from teen-agers seeking help.* And that was only in Los Angeles!

Television's "hidden persuaders," with their nonselective multi-million dollar advertising budgets, have done us all much harm, but television and magazines can be an effective counter weapon against the image of alcohol as the socially imperative beverage the brewers, vintners, and distillers want it to be. If we take lessons from Lucas Tanner and Sara T., parents can learn a lot. All it takes is a willingness to learn, and an open mind about the realities of teen-age drinking.

Some Hard Facts
About Drinks, Drinking,
and Being Drunk

The two most prevalent misconceptions, which adults seem to be harboring just as much as teen-agers, are that beer is a "milder" drink than hard liquor, and that a drunken person can be sobered up artificially. Here are the facts.

FACT: A can of beer is likely to be just as intoxicating as one mixed drink. "Ounce for ounce"—as some misguided researchers state—beer *is* milder, because of its lower *proof*, but who drinks beer by the ounce? A twelve-ounce can of beer has the same amount of alcohol as five ounces of table wine, three ounces of sherry or port, one ounce of whiskey, or one highball or cocktail. Anyone who thinks he is drinking "only beer" so he'll get less intoxicated is kidding himself and is in grave danger of becoming suddenly drunk.

FACT: When you pour hot black coffee into a drunken person, all you get is a wide-awake drunk. A cold shower gives you a wet drunk, and a walk in the cold night air will probably get you a chilly drunk. What makes a person drunk is his blood alcohol concentration (BAC), legally a 0.1 percent limit in most sobriety tests. *Coffee or cold showers do not dilute the BAC*. The only purpose in having a cup of coffee before driving home after a night of drinking is simply to *avoid having another drink*—not to sober up. The only sobering effect of a cold shower is that one isn't drinking while he's in it, although sometimes the ''shock'' gets some adrenalin moving and causes a temporary alertness.

FACT: It normally takes about one and a half hours for the body to burn up or eliminate the alcohol in a standard drink—be it a beer, a glass of wine or a highball. Hence, for each new drink consumed in that time, another one and a half hours is required to sober up. In other words, if you take three or four drinks in one hour, you'll need from four to six hours to get ''sober'' again. (And we are speaking here about body chemistry—not about the psychological factors that make some people act drunker than others.)

FACT: Alcohol is an addictive drug, just as much as heroin or cocaine are. What takes the ''drug'' stigma off alcohol for many people is the fact that it's legal. Being drunk is merely being overdosed on the drug alcohol.

FACT: The purpose of diluting drinks (with water, tonic, orange juice, etc.) is so you'll drink more slowly, not to decrease alcohol's intoxicating potency. Swallowing a shot of vodka is just as intoxicating as casually drinking a screwdriver, but the latter takes longer, and probably slows down the rate of consumption. *Mixed drinks (and beer and wine) get you just as drunk as straight booze, but more slowly*. Also, mixes make the taste of alcohol more palatable.

FACT: Alcohol doesn't require any digestion; it passes almost immediately to the small intestine where it is absorbed directly into the blood. That's the *only* reason taking food when drinking slows the intoxication process—the food creates a ''mash'' with the alcohol and gives the body more chance to burn it off before getting into your bloodstream and eventually your brain.

FACT: Alcohol is a *depressant*, not a stimulant. Most experts advise drinking only when you are happy. Drinking when depressed makes a person even more depressed, and depressed people become erratic. Statistics show that fights, murders, rows with police and neighbors, family arguments—all are most often connected with persons who have been drinking.

FACT: The "proof" number on a bottle of alcoholic beverage represents twice the alcohol strength. Hence, "100 proof" on a bottle of liquor means it is 50 percent pure alcohol.

FACT: Statistically, the highest proportion of drinking problems is among men in their early 20s, *not* the stereotyped skid row bum. The second highest incidence is in men between 40 and 50.

FACT: There is no such thing as "holding your liquor." People who seem to drink without getting drunk have merely developed a tolerance for alcohol, and tolerance is often a form of early dependence. Good ol' Joe who can really hold his drinks can get just as drunk as you, except that it costs him more and means he probably has a drinking problem already.

FACT: Mixing drinks does *not* make a person drunker, or drunk faster. It only makes a person sicker, simply because of mixing the different sugar-based chemicals which are used to cover up the inherent taste of alcohol.

FACT: Alcohol is *not* a sexual stimulant. It may stimulate *interest* in sex by depressing one's "conscience," but because it depresses the nervous system, it interferes with one's ability to perform. Drunks are lousy lovers.

FACT: Alcohol doesn't make you "warm" on a chilly night. Alcohol dilates the small blood vessels near the surface of the skin, which leads to a greater supply of blood in the surface areas, resulting in a *feeling* of warmth and a flushed skin—which actually results in a greater loss of body heat.

FACT: If you drink moderately (defined as less than two average-sized mixed drinks per day), it is unlikely that your liver will be permanently harmed in any way.

FACT: Alcohol can *both* make you fat *and* cause malnutrition at the same time. It has no food value at all, but if taken with an ordinary diet can actually lead to weight gain because the body uses the alcohol calories for energy immediately while storing your food calories as fat. On the other hand, alcohol also interferes with the absorption of certain vitamins and amino acids, and thus can contribute to vitamin and protein deficiency in heavy drinkers.

FACT: There is evidence that some drinks do, indeed, cause more of a hangover than others. Researchers at Rutgers University have measured more congeners (the breakdown products of alcohol and the flavoring and coloring agents) in bourbon than in vodka, *almost 100 times more*. These substances can alter brain waves by themselves, and mixing drinks can raise the percentage of congeners in your system.

FACT: In the alcohol-calorie game, most people tend to forget to count the calories in mixers. Two *shots* of gin will provide you with about 150 calories; but if you use a sixteen-ounce bottle of tonic to mix the gin with, you add about 200 more calories. Consequently two gin-and-tonics deliver about 350 calories, not 150.

Dr. Rex Wiederanders, a prominent American surgeon, describes the effect of alcohol on the body. Because cirrhosis of the liver receives the most publicity these days, the liver, naturally, is the organ most associated with drinking problems and alcoholism. However, alcohol's debilitating effects are numerous; it attacks on many fronts. Herewith, Dr. Wiederanders' short course on the physiology of alcohol, so parents can answer questions the next time they are asked:

Alcohol is a poison or toxin. It has short-term and long-term effects that are generally predictable. Of course, there is some difference in individual tolerance, but the effects are about the same in each drinker and rather rigidly related to the amount drunk. Small amounts, two drinks, two beers, two glasses of wine, bring relaxation, freshen the flow of conversation and enhance social intercourse. Four to six drinks and the speech is slowed, the reflexes retarded, control of the mind and body is shaken. It takes a man about twice as long to react to a given situation. More than this brings progressive loss of control and finally a state of sleep much deeper than ordinary—so deep it borders on anesthesia. An evening of drinking brings total lack of control followed by a poisoned morning: headache, vomiting, nausea, exhaustion.

To argue with a young person that by age 40 or 50 such-and-such will happen is fruitless. At 17, 40 is an eternity away. Who cares that about 20,000 cells die in the brain with each good drunk? These cells cannot regenerate, but what are a few thousand cells when the brain has billions? And so what if the nerves that carry impulses from the arms and legs to the brain and back again are susceptible to alcohol—peculiarly susceptible, so that when they die they hurt with sharp, screaming pains like lightning bolts, and the muscles they serve get flabby and the man walks with a funny, rubbery gait, just a little away from falling.

Forget the liver, struggling along to break down this poison, filling itself up with fat in the process, sacrificing its own cells to save the body. Forget these cells; the liver can grow more. In the process, unfortunately, so much scar tissue will form that it will itself kill more liver cells, but what's a little cirrhosis? What if the belly swells until the man looks ten months pregnant and the limbs get to be skinny, trembly sticks and he looks like a fat apple stuck on a toothpick? And the skin turns yellow and dry and he itches all over and there is no drug that will put out that fire?

And forget the third major target—the pancreas. If you think your pancreas is not hurt by alcohol, try eating a thick, greasy pork chop the morning after a great drunk. But the pancreas can survive until it spills its enzymes into the body and digests its own cells in a fulminating pancreatitis that literally eats out the organ itself and flows into the body cavity, burning a hole into the stomach or the bowels and blackening the gut as if it had been toasted in a fire.

All this can be forgotten. It is ten, fifteen, twenty years further down the alcoholic road.

But it's hard to forget those hangovers *now* or the night some punk half your size whipped the living hell out of you because you could not get your arms and legs going at the same time. For a lot of young people it will be impossible to forget an accident caused by drinking that left a number of injured, crippled, or dead. And it may be hard to forget that the girl or boy you really like is not with the ''in'' crowd.

Defining Your Own Attitudes About Drinking

You are the reflection in your children's eyes. A parent concerned about his children's drinking habits—or even *whether* his children drink in the first place—cannot help but be concerned about his own drinking habits.

Professional counselors will tell you that when you ask the average person to change his drinking habits, he will immediately get defensive. *Why* should I change, *I* don't drink too much! I can handle my drinking! We're talking about my kids, not about me! In fact, Americans are famous for spending huge sums of money *studying* a particular problem, but once the problem is identified, they don't know what to do about it, so they ignore it. Unfortunately, our children's drinking *attitudes* reflect our own.

The sad thing about teen-age drinking problems is that parents themselves find it difficult to define the problem; their own drinking patterns cloud the issue. We make excuses in the name of social drinking, but yet, as one expert put it, every time a bottle is opened we seem to act as if a tournament has

started. We make excuses by hiding behind a strange vocabu-
lary: A person is never "drunk" or "overdosed on the drug
alcohol." He is stoned, high, three-sheets-to-the-wind, polluted, smashed, pissed, tanked, crashed, pie-eyed, feeling no
pain, soused, pickled, loaded, ripped, tipsy, boiled, oiled,
boozed, canned, lit, in his cups, potted, tight, and feelin' fine.
We call drunken brawls "cocktail parties," and "alcoholic"
is a term we use for anyone but ourselves—we only "drink
a lot" or are "problem drinkers," "social drinkers," "occa-
sional drinkers," or "capable drinkers." How can we ask
parents concerned about drugs to convince children of the
potency of alcohol when they won't even recognize their own
heavy social drinking problems?

It all begins months and years before the child even considers drinking. Research has repeatedly shown that cultural
conditioning is the most important factor in educating youngsters about alcohol. Aimee Beckmann, a senior at St. Joseph's
Academy in Des Moines, Iowa, had this to say:

> The attitude of parents is an extremely important factor in
> any person's decision to drink or abstain. If children are
> exposed to drinking in moderate amounts at home [in the
> case of parents who drink], or are taught that drinking is a
> matter of personal choice [in the case of the abstaining
> parent], they are likely to view drinking as a normal part
> of society. However, if parents present alcohol as a for-
> bidden fruit, their children are likely to opt for drinking
> as a sign of rebellion rather than as simply another facet
> of their culture.

Says Mary Traxler, a student at nearby Roosevelt High
School:

> It seems to me that the real problem is not that teen-agers
> drink, but that because of the environment society creates

for them, it's difficult for them to acquire the right kind of *attitude* toward drinking. Possibly the great danger is not that teen-agers drink, but that the adult world, in their anxiety to keep them safe, encourages them to drink in the wrong way. Perhaps, then, parents should give up thinking entirely in terms of *preventing* kids from drinking and instead teach them what they want and need to know about drinking. In turn, it would then make it such a natural part of social affairs that the idea of limits would automatically be involved.

Unfortunately, many parents are not willing to give up their own vice in favor of setting a better example for their children, and this "lip-service" morality undermines the respect of the teen-ager for the parent. Dr. William B. Terhune, medical director emeritus of the Silver Hill Foundation in New Canaan, Connecticut, in *The Safe Way to Drink—How to Prevent Alcohol Problems Before They Start*, (William Morrow and Company, 1968) states that "kids exist in a permissive world which offers no leadership, yet condemns them when they are wrong. . . . The only thing wrong with kids today is the lack of discipline *and* the poor examples of their elders." In his book, Dr. Terhune presents five rules for parents:
1. Use alcohol moderately yourself, and teach kids to respect it as a potentially dangerous drug.
2. Adults must have the conviction of ideals and the courage to enforce them on their children.
3. Parents must not accept the "destructive permissiveness" of modern psychology and education.
4. Enforce rules with understanding and love.
5. Teach kids to have self-respect and confidence.
Dr. Terhune also offers various tips for safe drinking, as a way to guard against excessive drinking. These include going to drinking parties late; "delaying" the first drink at a party; sipping, to "nurse" a drink for at least half an hour; setting a

limit beforehand on the number of drinks you will have; eating while drinking, even at the risk of gaining weight (it may force you to get some exercise); taking pride in being individualistic enough to refuse drinks when offered; substituting nonalcoholic beverages; and mixing weak drinks as a matter of routine.

There are dozens, even hundreds, of lists of questions and tests and comparison tables to help people determine whether they are "problem" drinkers or "excessive" drinkers or outright alcoholics. But most of these tests are specious—they contain questions that would make even the most temperate of persons seem to be a raving alcoholic. Questions like "Do you ever have more than three drinks at a party?" or "Have you ever wished your husband didn't drink?" cannot possibly provide answers which can lead to any useful information. However, some lists are good ones; they ask realistic questions and are not designed to "prove" that a person drinks too much or to corroborate a predetermined point of view. One such is the following:

1. Do you think and talk about drinking often?
2. Do you drink more now than you used to?
3. Do you sometimes gulp drinks?
4. Do you often take a drink to help you relax?
5. Do you drink when you are alone?
6. Do you sometimes forget what happened when you were drinking?
7. Do you keep a bottle hidden somewhere—at home or at work—for a quick pick-me-up?
8. Do you need a drink to have fun?
9. Do you ever start drinking without really thinking about it?
10. Do you ever drink in the morning to relieve a hangover?

According to the Jaycees' Operation THRESHOLD, if

you answer yes to four or more of these questions, you may be one of the 10,000,000 Americans with a drinking problem, and the chances are good that your children will be excessive drinkers, too. Because we know our children look to us for guidelines in many things, including acceptable social behavior and responsible drinking patterns, the responses to the above questions may also be a clear indicator of the problem we face in educating our children properly in their *own* drinking habits.

Researchers have shown that there are certain behavioral patterns in the low-risk groups of drinkers, and these, too, can be set down as a set of questions to determine whether you, as a parent, presently are reflecting the proper attitudes about drinking:

1. If you drink, do you present an example of moderation without lecturing or preaching?

2. Are there established "ground rules" for using alcohol in your family, whether explicit or implied, that are generally agreed upon by all?

3. Does the family consider excessive drinking an *un*acceptable way to behave? Do you look upon drunkenness with pity instead of humor? Do you express disapproval if a guest in your home drinks too much?

4. Do you consider drinking as neither virtuous nor evil, in the sense of placing moral importance on it at all?

5. Do you avoid using drinking as a yardstick for adult status, or masculinity, or other moral characteristics? Do you "admire" someone who doesn't drink?

6. Do you avoid attaching social significance to abstention from drinking? Are friends and relatives just as comfortable in your home when they are not drinking? Do you always offer nonalcoholic as well as alcoholic beverages to guests?

7. Is drinking usually a part of another activity, such as dining, instead of an activity in itself?

8. Do you yourself abstain from alcoholic beverages for protracted periods?

Evidence indicates that if you answered yes to most of these questions—preferably to all of them—then you are presenting sound and responsible drinking behavior patterns and attitudes to your children.

An important exercise in determining your attitudes toward your children lies in arriving at the proper definition of "discipline." Remember, discipline is not pushing people around. It doesn't necessarily involve physical admonishment or punishment at all. Discipline may be thought of as the act of creating disciples, and parents concerned about their children's drinking habits should examine whether they are making their children disciples, or just temporary hostages until they've grown and left the home.

Many experts agree about the importance of discipline. "Too few parents blow the whistle," reports Ronald C. Force, clinical coordinator of St. Francis Boys Homes. "Parents have confused 'democracy' with '*laissez faire*,' and in so doing have functionally abandoned their children. Parents are often not really adults themselves. they don't know what they are, and so they can't respond adequately to the kid movement."

Parents aren't the only ones who have to redefine their attitudes about discipline. All society has to stop coddling drinkers. In California, New Jersey, and many other states, a bartender who sells a drink to an underage kid with a false I.D. is guilty of a crime and could lose his license, his job, his source of income, and his reputation, while the kid with the phony I.D. is sent home with a reprimand. A 17-year-old boy in Trenton, racing at high speed from one bar to another, crashed into and killed a young working mother. The man who served him his beer could be crucified under the penal code, and the woman's husband and 15-month-old baby have to live with the tragedy for the rest of their lives. Yet the drunken youth got off scot free from juvenile court with only a fine. The parents, the law, the city officials, will blame everyone but the drunken kid.

"If one of my sons was picked up for aberrant behavior with alcohol," states Dr. Morris Chafetz, "and if they didn't know I was a psychiatrist but I lived in the right part of Boston, they would pat him on the behind and send him home with an admonition. But if it was the child of a lower economic group, they tend to arrest him into some kind of treatment program. And I think they'd be doing my kid a disservice while helping the other kid out." Many of the experts feel that parents must change their attitude about drinking to the point where *teen-agers must be made to suffer the consequences of their drinking*, when such action is called for. Only then, according to psychiatrists, will they realize the extent of their erratic drinking behavior, and appreciate the enormously dangerous drug they have been abusing.

This attitude was the underlying prescription in the *Sara T.* movie and *Lucas Tanner* show described earlier. A child who comes home drunk and vomits on himself while passing out on the floor cannot be taught anything by a parent who cleans him up, dresses him for bed, tucks him in, and acts the next day as if nothing had happened. Perhaps if the child were left lying in his own mess when he awoke the next morning, reeking, sick, absent from school, and embarrassed, a valuable lesson would be learned.

Tough advice? Sure it is. It takes a strong and realistic parent to permit the cops to keep his son in jail overnight or to leave a disheveled and sick daughter sleeping on the patio. But remember: if one episode won't necessarily get the child to admit he has a problem, then maybe the second or third time will. The child has to make the initial decision to seek help; only then will it work. What the parent has to learn—and it is far more difficult even than the *child's* decision—is to do nothing, to let the child suffer the consequences of his alcohol overdose, so that the message will strike home harder and with more lasting impact. You cannot *make* a child stop drinking.

As parents, you may ask, "But how can we prevent alcohol problems before they start?"

"A good look around, an analysis of the values surrounding your family should be the first step," advises psychologist Dr. Nathan Adler of the University of California. "The ads tell us to be urbane, to serve the proper gin and have a nice big house in a fashionable suburb, and parents aren't going to be able to overcome that overnight. It's a total issue." A constant reminder of all the elements involved in this "total issue" is a prerequisite for dealing with a drinking culture. And one of the critical elements is the demands we may be placing on our children to "achieve," to "accomplish" at such an early age that the psychological pressures become almost unbearable *without* drinking. The child who is a sports hero, for example, a young champion, the popular student who makes it with all the girls and for whom everything has been easy may be in danger later in life. Life may seem to go downhill for him, and social drinking may increasingly replace achievement. "He's blown it already," says Dr. Adler, "he can't go anywhere." On the other hand, the quiet child, the late maturer, the nonaggressive student who seems to be well-balanced both in thought and activities, is likely to be the person who is still achieving things in his 40s and 50s with little problem with alcohol.

The message here is for the parent *not* to place achievement stresses on his child, *not* to make demands to produce and to be on top of everything that comes along. Our culture seems to demand that we first-name everybody, attend large cocktail parties where we must talk to everyone for three minutes and remember everyone's name, be genial, urbane, and witty, look successful, and be what Dr. Adler calls "pseudo-intimate." In this milieu, alcohol is the homogenizing agent, the ingredient that makes it all easier to get through. Consequently, society has picked up alcohol as an accepted part of the achievement motive. But the fact is that the poor sad sack who is out of the mainstream and "rat race" is far less likely to have alcohol problems. This applies equally to children and to adults.

The concerned parent should know that *any* time a child gets drunk, there is a problem. The alcoholic isn't just the child who drinks every day, or gets drunk twice a weekend at parties or at drive-ins. The more frequently it happens, of course, the more serious it is, but *a child does not get drunk accidentally.* Even the kids we interviewed around the country will agree with this readily—the drunken teen-ager usually gets drunk *on purpose.* It's surely the sign of some kind of underlying problem, perhaps a problem-solving one in which the kid must take out some aggression as a result of the inner frustrations he is experiencing. Dr. Adler tells the story of the alcoholic, the pothead and the heroin addict at the locked gates of a city, trying to gain entry.

The alcoholic says, "Let's get a battering ram and beat the gate down!"

The heroin addict says, "Let's go to sleep and figure it out in the morning."

And the pothead says, "Let's go in through the keyhole!"

Parents should look at their children's drinking companions. The types of people a person drinks with influence his drinking behavior. Even the type of beverage is determined partly by your drinking companions. We aren't saying that "bad companions" may encourage your child to drink, but an underlying inferiority or negative self-feeling may be the reason your teen-ager "hangs around" with the type of friends who would encourage his drinking to excess.

If your child drinks, ask yourself where is the source of stress? Where does tension come from in his young life? What are your child's needs and how should they be met? Are they being met at all? If the child is drinking excessively, at whatever age, he is undoubtedly flying a small-craft warning. "What you do is change course," Dr. Adler advises. "You find out what the problem is and you deal with it accordingly. A problem drinker may have mental defects, he may be schizoid, he may be depressed, he may have flights from homosexuality, which terrifies him. Again, we have to identify the underlying cause. The alcohol is merely symptomatic."

How to Help Your Children Handle Booze

There are definite things we can do to help our children handle drinking. The most important thing to impress upon them is the fact that someday soon (probably around junior-high-school age), someone will invite them to take a drink. Perhaps they will even be urged to drink; the pressure may be great to "join the crowd." However, by the time the drink, or can of beer, is in the child's hand, it is too late for him to begin to consider whether, what, or how much he plans to drink that evening. That is a decision that must be made ahead of time, and it is the decision that will, in various forms, remain with him for the rest of his life.

Here are a few guidelines that may help prepare the child to make that decision sanely:

MAY I HAVE A SIP OF YOUR BEER, DAD?

Remembering that a twelve-ounce *can* of beer is nearly as potent as the average mixed drink, there is really nothing wrong with letting your child have a *sip* of beer. Small children are often intrigued by the taste of beer, and in some cases a sip or two may actually be good for them. In the case of mixed drinks, however, a request for a "taste" should be met with some kind of qualifying remark. You might warn the child that the taste will be a little harsh, or else remind him that you're aware that he probably won't like the taste of it. If the drink *is*, in fact, harsh, such as Kentucky bourbon on the rocks, then it may prove beneficial in the sense that the child's dislike for that taste may be established. In any case, you will have diminished the child's curiosity, and as long as you don't make a great issue of the request, you may enhance the image of drinking as a normal act and not as the beginning of a wild orgiastic spree.

WHEN DO I "TALK" TO MY CHILD ABOUT DRINKING?

As a rule of thumb, the sixth grade. The beginning of junior high school is generally acknowledged among experts to be the "danger zone" of a child's initiation to drinking and the start of great peer pressure. According to Dr. Robert A. Zucker of Rutgers University, the best time to start is when the child's ideals are "in a state of flux," ordinarily from 11 to 14 years of age. Most of the kids we spoke to seemed to agree —they would rather have had their parents get them "primed" for the drinking pressure at an earlier age, than have the Great Booze Discussion dropped on them *after* they've made a peer commitment.

TO DRINK OR NOT TO DRINK—HELPING YOUR CHILD DECIDE.

The primary thing to remember when discussing the *act* of drinking with your child is to get the point across that there *is* a decision to be made. The decision to make should not be whether to *accede*, to give in, to drinking, but whether drinking in the first place is a desirable *modus operandi*. Impress upon them the fact that deciding *not* to drink is a workable alternative.

HOW DO I INTRODUCE THE FIRST DRINK TO MY CHILD?

In the first place, wait until he asks. Don't sit down one day out of the blue and announce to your child that you will now conduct the Great Booze Discussion. This will create more confusion than confidence. Rather, when you feel that your child is approaching the alcohol experimentation period, remember that it is far better that he have the first drink in his home and under nonimperative conditions. The child should take his first drink in a comfortable situation. Dilute a small amount with water and ice—if it's hard booze—and be sure he takes it on a full stomach. If wine or beer, make it a small dose. Do *not* force it upon him; more harm than good has been done by parents who apply the old have-a-cigarette-and-choke-to-death theory to drinking. Getting your child intentionally drunk will accomplish nothing. Be sure you inform the child that alcohol is a drug, albeit a legal one, and that it should be treated as such. *Don't be afraid to sound "square!"*

THE FIRST PARTY—WHAT DO YOU SAY?

Once again, if a parent is even interested in the situation, he'll appreciate the need for common sense rather than formula advice. A child going to his first party should understand that *you* understand. There should be a fundamental trust working before the question comes up. Then, perhaps, a gentle reminder that perhaps there will be alcohol available, that maybe some kids will be doing their "macho" thing and *acting* drunk, that maybe some kids will bug other kids to drink, insisting that the party can't be "fun" if people don't drink. Remind them of the right *not* to drink, and of what you know yourself from observing your own drinking friends; the ones who *insist* you drink probably have a drinking problem themselves.

BUT MOM (DAD), IF I DON'T DRINK I CAN'T HAVE A GOOD TIME.

Here's the chance to bring up alcohol dependency. Most kids will understand that if they can't have a good time *without* alcohol, there is definitely a dependency problem. But most parents are loath to bring it up. "Dependency" is a troublesome word. It conjures visions of the skid-row bum, of begging in the streets, of Alcoholics Anonymous . . . of everything but what it *really* means. The parent should recall that asking a kid whether he can have a good time without drinking is *not* a stupid question. What's sad is not being *able* to ask it.

IF I DON'T DRINK, THEY'LL CALL ME A "FREAK."

"And if you do drink, they'll call you a drunk." Here, again, peer pressure is an important consideration. Make sure your child understands what peer pressure is before he gets into a situation where he's "expected" to drink. You can ask a child how much anesthesia he wants before he engages in a particular activity—how much he wants to be drugged. You can remind him that it isn't a crime to say "Thank you, no" to an offer, or that a cop will never think he's a "freak" when he's driving all his "groovy" friends home from the party. You can remind him of your faith in his good judgment. And you can remind him that drinking doesn't make a person sexier, taller, stronger, older, more sophisticated or more popular, unless he's impressing the wrong people to begin with.

THE TEEN-AGER WHO CAN "HANDLE" DRINKING.

Many adults know someone—an uncle, a friend, a cousin—who can drink everyone under the table. Usually, he's the guy who is singing his brains out by the piano, the "life of the party" kind of person who's drinking continuously and about whom everyone always seems to be remarking that he can hold his booze. Well, it may be hard to realize, but if your child ever tells you he can "handle" his drinking, he's likely to become that obnoxious red-nosed life of the party most of us would like to avoid. "Handling" alcohol merely means a tolerance has been built up—which in turn means that the man can become just as drunk, but has learned either not to display the fact, or else has gone so far over the edge that his dependency *requires* that he drink more than normal before he reacts. Either way, alcohol is handling *him*, and your teen-ager should know the distinction.

YOU DRINK, FOLKS, SO IT MUST BE OKAY FOR ME!

Have you ever seen a truly fat man? An obese man? If you have, ask your child whether that man's child ever asked him, "Dad, *you're* fat, so why can't *I* be fat?" Don't let your child put you on the defensive because you drink. If you drink *too much*, that's something else. Maybe you'd better reexamine your own drinking habits. But if you have established that a few drinks are harmless, or that drinking, *per se*, bears no stigma, then your child cannot point to your behavior to justify his own.

A magazine once asked Dr. Chafetz whether he had had any problems in his own family. After admitting that there had been a few episodes, he told how his kids, when small, and knowing that he treated alcoholism in his practice, used to tell their teachers that their daddy was "an alcoholic doctor."

HAVING A PARTY AND WANTING TO SERVE BEER.

Who decides this, after all? Does your child tell you what will be served at a party, or is it subject to *your* decision? The best attitude toward this problem is the family's empathy with the guests' parents. Do you want *your* children served beer (or whatever) when they attend a party elsewhere? Are you responsible for getting the guests home after the party if they have "a little too much to drink?" Who makes the decision depends on your particular family structure. Will your child respect your reply if you insist that *no* beer be served? And if he won't, then isn't there a more basic problem to confront than whether he'll serve beer at a party? Also, are you, the parent, aware of the fact that it is probably against the law in your state to serve alcoholic beverages to any child other than your own? The laws vary from state to state, and it would probably be a good idea to acquaint yourself with your local laws and the punishments for breaking them. Once again, here is a lesson in "being square." The "cool parent" will let his children have their way and serve beer at the party. But if one of the teen-agers is killed on the way home because he had too much to drink, it won't be the "square" parent who is losing sleep.

WHAT TO TELL A CHILD ABOUT GETTING INTO A CAR WITH A DRINKING DRIVER.

Do you want to risk being physically handicapped for the rest of your life? How would you feel if you were a passenger in a car that crashed head-on into another car and killed other people? It's just as stupid to ride with a drinking driver as it is to stand up in a roller coaster.

WHAT TO TELL A DATE WHO DRINKS TOO MUCH.

Kids these days place a high value on being up-front, honest and "straight." If your child knows the real value in saying something like "Hey, you're a little smashed and I just don't want to have to hassle with that," then he's come a long way already.

Afterword

There are literally hundreds—perhaps thousands—of pamphlets, brochures and books on the subject of alcoholism —how to recognize it, what to know about it, what to do about it and learning to live with it. Alcoholics Anonymous itself has published more than fifty, and the National Institute on Alcohol Abuse and Alcoholism, the National Council on Alcoholism, Inc., various state departments of public health and local communities and agencies probably contribute hundreds more, not to mention the American Medical Association, smaller medical associations, private rehabilitation centers, religious and service organizations, civic agencies, private foundations, and major universities and colleges around the nation. There is no paucity of publications, from the extremely basic to the highly technical, about the "illness" of excess drinking. To simply list in alphabetical order their names and addresses would not really be the service it might appear to be. Anyone who is even remotely close to a drinker, young or old, has heard of some place to turn, whether it be the Yellow Pages for the local A.A. number or the name of a good psychiatrist, minister, or doctor.

There is, however, a lot to be gained from knowing where to find important information without having to wade through a ream of sermons or simplistic pamphlets describing cirrhosis of the liver. The following list provides that information.

We believe these publications—most of which are either free or available for less than a dollar—will give the concerned parent more than ample preliminary preparation for becoming more involved in the number-one health problem among teenagers today. Most libraries, too, have a whole shelf of books dealing with alcoholism.

One of the purposes of this book is to help bring the literature of *teen-age* drinking out of the Dark Ages. In this decade when men walk on the moon but when millions of dollars more are spent annually on pet food than on drug abuse and rehabilitation, we hope our book will give new meaning to the phrase "Thank God he's not on drugs."

PAMPHLETS:

"Alcoholics and Alcoholism"
    available from:
    Public Affairs Pamphlets
    381 Park Avenue South
    New York, NY 10016

Afterword

"Alcohol in Our Society"
North Dakota Commission on Alcoholism
State Capitol
Bismarck, ND 58501
"Alcoholism"
Superintendent of Documents
U.S. Government Printing Office
Washington, D.C. 20402
"Alcohol and the Adolescent"
"13 Steps to Alcoholism"
"Strictly for Teenagers"
   all three above—plus articles and pamphlets too
   numerous to list can be obtained by writing to:
   National Council on Alcoholism
   2 Park Avenue
   New York, NY 10016
"Alcohol—Do You Know Enough About It?"
"It's My Life"
"Coffee, Tea and Me"
   above three available from:
   Addiction Research Foundation of Ontario
   33 Russell Street
   Toronto, Ontario M5S 2S1
"Alcohol: A Family Affair"
   National Congress of Parents and Teachers
   700 North Rush Street
   Chicago, IL 60611
"An Important Question"
   Director of Public Education—State of Florida
   Bureau of Alcoholic Rehabilitation
   P.O. Box 1147
   Avon Park, FL 33825

"A B C's of Drinking and Driving"
"Social Drinking—For People Who Drink and People Who
Don't . . . "
"Drinking Myths—A Guided Tour Through Folklore, Fan-
tasy, Humbug and Hogwash"
above three available from:
Operation THRESHOLD
United States Jaycees
Box 7
Tulsa, OK 74102

"The New Alcoholics: Teenagers" by Jules Saltman
Public Affairs Pamphlets
381 Park Avenue South
New York, NY 10016

"Juice Use" by Sol Gordon and Roger Conant
Ed-U Press
Syracuse University Institute for Family Research and Edu-
cation
760 Ostrom Avenue
Syracuse, NY 13210

"Thinking About Drinking"
U.S. Department of Health, Education and Welfare
National Institute on Alcohol Abuse and Alcoholism
Superintendent of Documents
U.S. Government Printing Office
Washington, D.C. 20402

"How Alcohol Affects the Body"
"What the Body Does With Alcohol"
"What Shall We Teach the Young About Drinking?"
above three available from:
Rutgers Center of Alcohol Studies—Publications Di-
vision
Rutgers University
New Brunswick, NJ 08903

"When Ethyl Takes the Wheel"
"I've Got Ethyl on My Mind"
"Myths About Drinking"
"More Myths About Drinking"
"I Can't Be an Alcoholic Because...."
"Is There Room for Ethyl?"
"Teen-age Drinking and Driving"
  all of the above available from:
  Michigan Alcohol Education Foundation
  Box 212
  Lansing, MI 48902

Alcoholics Anonymous
  numerous pamphlets and booklets are available at your local
  A.A. office—there are too many to list here.

BOOKLETS

Alcohol and Health
  U.S. Department of Health, Education and Welfare
  Public Health Service
  National Institute on Alcohol Abuse and Alcoholism
  5600 Fishers Lane
  Rockville, MD 20852
Learning About Alcohol–A Resource Book for Teachers
  American Association for Health, Physical Education and
  Recreation
  1201 Sixteenth Street, N.W.
  Washington, D.C. 20036

Teaching About Beverage Alcohol
State of Illinois
Office of the Superintendent of Public Instruction
302 State Office Building
Springfield, IL 62706

Alternative Pursuits for America's 3rd Century
A Resource Book on Alternatives to Drugs
National Institute on Drug Abuse
11400 Rockville Pike
Rockville, MD 20852

INFORMATION SOURCES—AGENCIES
AND ORGANIZATIONS

Alcoholics Anonymous World Services, Inc.
Box 459, Grand Central Station
New York, NY 10017

Al-Anon Family Group Headquarters
Post Office Box 182
Madison Square Station
New York, NY 10010

Health Education—Division of Instruction
Office of the Superintendent of Public Instruction
316 South Second Street
Springfield, IL 62706

Licensed Beverage Industries, Inc.
155 East 44th Street
New York, NY 10017

Michigan Council on Alcohol Problems
728 West Allegany
Lansing, MI 48902

National Council on Alcoholism, Inc.
2 Park Avenue
New York, NY 10016

North American Association on Alcoholism Programs
1130 17th Street N.W.
Washington, D.C. 20036

National Transportation Safety Board
Department of Transportation
Washington, D.C. 20591

Rutgers Center of Alcohol Studies
Rutgers University
New Brunswick, NJ 08903

Section on Alcoholism Programs
Department of Mental Health
401 South Spring Street
Springfield, IL 62706

The Christopher D. Smithers Foundation
405 Park Avenue
New York, NY 10022

Appendix:
The Toronto Report

This study (see Chapter 1) was one of a series taken in metropolitan Toronto, first in 1968 and repeated every two years since then. Each study, except for 1970 when grade 6 was included, sampled students in grades 7, 9, 11, and 13. And it should be noted that this study was not taken of a dozen, or two dozen, or a hundred or a few hundred students. The study included, in 1972, 6,641 students, and in 1974 almost 3,500 students. No one can debate whether the Toronto study was a representative sampling—in our search for the most up-to-date and comprehensive literature on alcoholism research among the younger generation, we found no survey in existence which even approached the Toronto survey for sheer thoroughness and extent of subjects sampled. The survey was taken among students with parental permission to fill out candid questionnaires and was administered by trained interviewers not connected in any way with staffs of local schools. The questionnaires were anonymous, and where appropriate, letters of permission for parents were translated into Greek, Ukrainian, Italian, Polish, Portuguese, and Chinese. Finally, the information sought included demographic characteristics (age, sex, grade, father's occupation, etc.), prevalence and frequency of alcohol use, sources of information about drugs, attitudes toward alcohol and other drugs and drug users, a sampling of knowledge about drugs, and a correlation with drinking and driving habits.

The results of the Toronto survey, as with so many other surveys and studies in recent years, would cause weeping and gnashing of teeth within the Distilled Spirits Council of the United States, Inc., who insist that teen-age drinking is not on the rise. Of the drugs sampled, "only the use of alcohol, marijuana and glue increased significantly between 1972 and 1974." The prevalence table for Grades 7, 9, 11, and 13 shows the following drug use (numbers indicate percent of students):

	1968	1970	1972	1974
Alcohol	46.3	60.2	70.6	72.9
Marijuana	6.7	18.3	20.9	22.9
Glue	5.7	3.8	2.9	3.8

All the other drugs sampled either were not increased in usage or else their increase was not judged "significant." Clearly, the increase in use of alcohol among 3,500 students went from 46.3 percent to 72.9 percent over the course of six years—*an increase of 26.6 percent.*

Of the almost 3,500 students sampled in 1970, 2.0 percent reported they drank every day—or about 70 students. In 1972, 23.3 percent reported drinking four times a month or more, compared with an increase to 24.5 percent in 1974.

Some other random results:

—male users of alcohol and marijuana tended to take these drugs more frequently than females (at odds with several other studies which show a markedly more rapid rise in female teen-age drinking than male).

—alcohol use increased with grade level; only 51.5 percent of Grade 7 students drank alcohol, compared with 92.6 percent in Grade 13.

—use of alcohol was *low* among students with high grade averages and low grade averages. More than 77 percent of the students with average marks were excessive drinkers. *Since most parents consider their kids average students, this would underscore the need for closer attention to your children's drinking behavior and your own influence on that behavior within the family environment.*

Appendix

—the use of alcohol, marijuana and barbiturates was highest among students whose fathers were in professional or managerial occupations. In 1972, only alcohol was highest among children of professional or management fathers. (It's interesting to note that other surveys indicate that professional or management fathers are among the heaviest drinkers.)

—all previous surveys showed that information about drugs was gotten most often from the mass media, while the second most important source was "kids I hang around with." Church and school, family or personal experiences, were much less often mentioned as sources from which information was acquired about drugs. In 1974, a greater proportion of users of tobacco, alcohol, marijuana, and glue acquired their information from "kids I hang around with," than did nonusers of these drugs.

And finally, one of the major conclusions of the Toronto report: "Alcohol use, in particular, now involves almost 73 percent of the students in Grades 7, 9, 11 and 13 . . . " and that ". . . alcohol and marijuana use do not seem to be leveling off."

HV
5135
A33

Addeo, Edmond
    G. 1936—

Why our children
drink